CW00368913

A SPORTING ALMANAC

GOLF

A SPORTING ALMANAC

GOLF

Photographs by the
Daily Mail

E. Balmer

© Atlantic Publishing 2003

First published in the UK in 2003
exclusively for
WHSmith Limited, Greenbridge Road, Swindon SN3 3LD
www.WHSmith.co.uk

Produced by Atlantic Publishing
.All photographs © Associated Newspapers Archive

All rights reserved.
No part of this publication may be reproduced or transmitted in any form or
by any means, electronic or mechanical, including photocopying, recording,
or any information storage and retrieval system, without permission in
writing from the copyright holders.

A catalogue record for this book is available from the British Library.

ISBN 0 9545267 0 8
Printed in China

The Royal Birkdale Golf Club, Southport, Lancashire, England

CONTENTS

The rise of the game 6
The R&A 8
The international game 10
Professionals and amateurs 11
The modern game 12
Hall of fame 14
The contenders 58
Classic courses 70
Major competitions 90
The Open Championship 92
The US Open Championship 96
The Masters Tournament 100
The USPGA Championship 102
The Ryder Cup 104
Women in golf 114
Golfing miscellany 118

THE RISE OF THE GAME

T here is some dispute as to the true origins of the game. Was an early form of golf the game played in Holland under the name 'kolven'? What about the French claim with their ancient game 'jeu de mail'? Perhaps one of the things the Romans did do for us was bequeath their game 'paganica'. Ultimately there is no documentary evidence as to its true origins, perhaps golf was a game that evolved over time, being slowly shaped and perfected by earnest sportsmen.

There were a number of different stick and ball games played throughout early Europe and any one of these could be a forerunner of today's game. What we know of paganica is limited; it was played with a bent stick and a feather stuffed, leather ball. In the ancient Flemish game of 'chole', the clubs used were made of wood with iron heads. The game is played in teams and the object is to hit the ball with the club at a far distant target, perhaps a marked tree or a post. One team has three strokes to get the ball forward; the opposing team is then given the opportunity to hit the same

ball back towards the start or into a hazard, anything to prevent their rivals from succeeding. 'Jeu de mail' is limited to being played in a court and in principle the rules are closer to those of golf. Rather than a team game, players compete as individuals, striking their ball with a wooden mallet to hit a specified target. They keep their own ball throughout and the winner is the player who requires the least number of strokes to hit the target. 'Kolven' or 'colf' is again played on a course, however the condition of the course can vary; it can be played on wooden courts, outside on turf, even on ice. Initially the targets were four doors, but these were eventually substituted by holes in the ground, with a pole protruding. Each of these games could be viewed as an early form of golf (or even of croquet or hockey). They share certain obvious characteristics to the modern game.

It is to Scotland, however, that we look for the first recorded evidence of golf itself. In 1457, King James II declared that 'Fute-ball and Golfe be utterly cryit doune, and nocht usit'. Why was golf banned? It was already so popular that young men were too busy putting a few holes to get down to the serious business of practising their archery and other martial skills, a distinct advantage to the English army lurking over the border. The ban was finally lifted in 1502. The game gradually became popular on both sides of the border, and with both sexes. The first course to be set up in England was at Blackheath in London in 1608. It was apparently built by the homesick Scottish courtiers of James VI of Scotland who had recently become James I of England. The oldest golf club in the world is, however, back in Scotland. The Honourable Company of Edinburgh Golfers were in 1744 located at Leith, from there they moved to Musselburgh and finally to Muirfield, where their descendants remain to this day.

Below: Sir Henry Cotton and James Braid during a professional tournament at High Barnet in 1927. Opposite page: Old Tom Morris (second from left) and Allan Robertson (third from right) at St Andrews.

THE R&A

In 1522, a licence was granted to the people of St Andrews, permitting them to play at 'golf, futball, schuteing' and rear rabbits on the links. By 1754, the Society of St. Andrews Golfers, '22 Noblemen and Gentlemen of the Kingdom of Fife', were regularly gathering to play and enjoy convivial drinking and eating. The Society would compete annually in its own competition using the rules devised by the Edinburgh golfers at Leith. In 1764, they had an 18-hole course constructed, which has since become standard and in 1834 the club was honoured by William IV, who became their patron. The title of Royal & Ancient Golf Club of St Andrews was conferred and their new club house was erected twenty years later.

With Royal patronage, a fine course and its own new set of rules, the R&A, as it is commonly known, was to become the governing body of the game, administering golf from the fine clubhouse which still dominates the Old course. Today the R&A has four areas of responsibility: upholding the rules and acting as arbiter in any dispute; the administration of the Open Championship and other key events; the profits earned from these are then channelled into the development of the game worldwide; and finally, operating as a private club with currently over 2000 members.

Below: The grand club house at St Andrews.

Opposite page: View across the 15th fairway and green.

THE INTERNATIONAL GAME

A s the British Empire grew in the eighteenth and nineteenth centuries, so the British took their sports and pastimes with them. As a result, golf began its gradual spread across the globe. The first golf club outside Britain was in Bangalore, India, which opened in 1820. The Royal Calcutta and the Royal Bombay soon followed. By the end of the nineteenth century, clubs could be found in France, Canada, Australia, South Africa and Hong Kong.

Golf was first introduced to America by Scottish officers fighting in the War of Independence during the late eighteenth century. Two clubs were formed in the Deep South, the South Carolina Golf Club in 1786 and in Georgia, the Savannah Golf Club built in 1796. Although these clubs are recognised as the oldest, interest in the sport didn't last. It wasn't until a century later that golf would grasp the imagination of the United States.

The 'father of golf' in the US was another expatriate Scot, from Fife near St Andrews. John Reid was a resident of Yonkers, New York and had ordered a set a clubs from Old Tom Morris's shop in St Andrews; his intention was to introduce the game to friends. In 1888, Reid and five of his friends played an historic first round on a cow pasture close to Reid's home, where they laid out a three hole course. Later that same year they moved to a larger site and formed the St Andrew's Golf Club, named after the links course in Scotland. Golf had arrived in America.

Below: Old Tom Morris's shop sold hand-crafted clubs and balls.

In 1894, six of the newly established clubs formed the United States Golf Association (USGA) and elected as their president, Theodore Havermeyer. The following year the USGA held the first US Open and US Amateur Championships. The association was entrusted with regulating the game in the United States and Mexico, a role it still holds to this day. The game eventually attracted the attention of the media which raised its profile enormously. In 1897 the monthly magazine, 'Golf', was published in the US and by the turn of the century there were over 1000 clubs across the country.

PROFESSIONALS & AMATEURS

Golf was a gentleman's game and gentlemen were amateurs. Professional golfers were there to provide services to the club players. They made their living by betting against their opponents, by carrying clubs and bags and occasionally by tutoring. Golfers were warned against betting with professionals, they were advised not to buy them drinks at the end of rounds, in short, not to encourage them in anyway. Pros were not permitted to enter the clubhouses, a practice that continued well into the twentieth century. In 1860, the first British Open Championship was held at Prestwick in Scotland, a competition that remains open to both amateurs and professionals.

Below: Walter Hagen makes a speech after America won the Ryder Cup in 1937.

The prejudice against professionals was far greater in Britain than in the United States, where greater financial incentives in the sport had led to a proliferation of professional players. When the American star professional Walter Hagen travelled to Britain during the 1920s he was determined to upset the golfing class system. Hagen was a good example of a superior player who would not be treated as an inferior. He refused to enter the clubhouse for the ceremony following the 1923 Open at Troon because he and his colleagues had been refused entry at the start of the tournament. Now of course, the professional players are the sporting heroes, a far cry from the early days of the game.

THE MODERN GAME

here are now four Major tournaments in the annual golf calendar, the British and US Opens, the US Majors and the US PGA. These are the tournaments that top level players aspire to succeed in, the more Masters they accumulate the more likely they are to be considered 'great'. Only one golfer to date has achieved a 'Grand Slam' of four Majors in one year, Bobby Jones, although his titles were in fact the British and US Opens, and the British and US Amateurs in 1930, meaning that his feat can never be repeated. The other important golfing event is the biennial Ryder Cup Championship, played originally between the USA and Britain, and now the USA and Europe. The Ryder Cup has become enormously successful in recent years, for a number of reasons explored later.

Television coverage of the Majors and other key tournaments has had a huge impact on the game. Golf can now reach audiences in all corners of the globe and media attention has resulted in an inevitable rise in corporate sponsorship. As a consequence of this golf has become not only a global enterprise but, at the top level a highly lucrative one. In 1968, Arnold Palmer became the first player to amass earnings of $1million. In recent years Tiger Woods has become the game's top money earner and at the end of 2002 he had accumulated over $33 million. Woods's fortune has been further supplemented by his deal with sports equipment manufacturer, Nike.

Below: American golfer Arnold Palmer in 1961.

Opposite page: One of the newer golfing stars, Tiger Woods.

HALL of FAME

This Hall of Fame not only includes the great champions,
but also the players who have made a significant
contribution to the history of the game. While there is
always much debate about just who are the greats of golf
- both past and present - it is likely that most enthusiasts
would feature all the outstanding golfers profiled here.

THE MAJORS

Majors: 5

Masters   1980, 1983

The Open: 1979, 1984
              1988

SEVERIANO BALLESTEROS

1957-

Born in Pedrena, Spain, Seve Ballesteros taught himself to play golf as a child with only one club, a three iron. Since then he has clocked up a total of 52 titles, among them three times British Open champion, in 1979, 1984 and 1988, and twice US Masters winner, in 1980 and 1983. Ballesteros's ability to execute inventive and improbable shots to help him out of a tight spot is legendary and probably due to those early days playing with his brothers. His style often resulted in errant drives and he earned himself the nickname 'The Car Park Champion' at Lytham St Annes in 1979 after he played his second at the 16th hole from among the cars. When he became the youngest ever player to win the Masters at the age of 23, he forfeited a massive lead by visiting the water in two rounds Despite this he is undoubtedly one of the greatest golfers ever to have played and was certainly the most formidable of opponents during the 1980s.

Ballesteros's role in revitalising the game in Europe cannot be ignored. He became the first European to don the green blazer when he won the US Masters in 1980 and was also instrumental in reviving the fortunes of Europe's Ryder Cup team. In 1985, along with five other Spanish golfers, including Jose Olazabal, he spearheaded what was to become known as the 'Spanish Armada', but instead of defeat, they helped Europe steal a crucial victory from the Americans. Ballesteros went on to play in a further seven Ryder Cup tournaments and eventually captained the side to a dramatic victory at Valderrama in 1997.

Below: Ballesteros holds aloft the famous trophy, after winning the British Open in 1979.

Legend has it that he was born to play golf, gifted with a right arm longer than the left that improved his game. Certainly a passionate and charismatic character, both on and off the course, his style and skill made Seve one of golf's most enduring and popular stars.

HENRY COTTON

1907-1987

Henry Cotton was one of the influential figures in British golf and is often credited with pulling the British game into the modern era. The public school educated son of a wealthy industrialist, Cotton was a talented and charismatic player who instigated better fees and privileges for pros. American golfers had dominated the sport and enjoyed lavish treatment that British golfers could only dream of. It was Henry Cotton who, having crossed the Atlantic as a 22-year-old Ryder Cup contender in 1929, demanded to be accorded the same treatment as the Americans.

Often referred to as the 'British Walter Hagen', Cotton was a flamboyant golfer who appreciated the potential of commercial endorsement. He was associated with the equipment maker Dunlop, who famously christened his ball the '65' after he played what many described as 'perfect golf' in the second round of the Open Championship 1934, shooting 65. He was an outspoken and confident personality, traits that sometimes proved to be detrimental to his popularity. In 1949 he refused his place on the Ryder Cup team, not wishing be captained by Charles Whitcombe. His often controversial comments in the press accorded him some criticism; but did bring a greater level of interest in the sport.

Below: In 1937, Cotton won the British Open for the second time. Opposite page: When he was still only 20, Cotton finished 9th in the Open.

Ultimately, however, Cotton was a great sportsman with a natural talent for the game. He won three British Open titles in 1934, 1937 and 1948 and, had it not been for the interruption caused by the Second World War, he may well have increased this total. Cotton was also vital in securing Britain's victory in the 1929 Ryder Cup, scoring the winning points against Al Watrous, and he went on to captain the side in 1953.

A founding member of the Golf Foundation, Cotton was the first player to be knighted for his services to the sport. No wonder, then, that he earned the nickname, 'the maestro'.

THE MAJORS

Majors: 3

The Open: 1934, 1937, 1948

THE MAJORS

Majors:	6
Masters:	1989, 1990, 1996
The Open:	1987, 1990 1992

NICK FALDO

1957 –

Considered to be one of Britain's finest ever golfers, Nick Faldo is an example of what dedication and focus can do for a sports professional. He famously claimed to have been inspired by Jack Nicklaus's 1972 Masters victory and by 1976 had turned professional, having been Britain's youngest-ever amateur champion. Although naturally talented, Faldo enlisted the help of a coaching guru David Leadbetter to enable him to reap more titles. The result: an improved swing. The cost of this swing change was four years in the golfing wilderness, but when Faldo won the British Open in 1987 he had at last made his mark on the world scene and would continue to do so for the next ten years.

Faldo has collected titles and records aplenty and it is this that maintains his status as Britain's most successful golfer. He went on to win the Open twice more, in 1990 at St Andrews and again in 1992 at Muirfield. 1990 was a particularly good year for Faldo: he took the Masters at Augusta for the second time, having won it the year before, and so became only the second man to win in successive years - the first being his hero Nicklaus. He went on to win the Masters again in 1996, staging a terrific comeback to beat Greg Norman after being six strokes behind going into the last day.

It is however, for his Ryder Cup record that he is particularly admired. He has played in more Ryder Cup tournaments than anyone else, a record 11, which includes membership of four winning teams. His first appearance in the European team came when he was only 20-years-old, the second youngest player ever. So many appearances mean that Faldo also holds the record for the most points scored (25) the most holes played (766) and the most wins (23), although these impressive statistics could not have been attained without considerable talent.

Becoming the first British golfer to win over £1million in a season, Faldo has truly earned his place as one of golf's big players.

Below: Faldo lines up a shot.
Opposite page: In action during the Ryder Cup in 1991.

WALTER HAGEN

1892 – 1969

Born in New York, Walter Hagen's successes as a golfer were overshadowed by his character. A larger-than-life showman, Hagen's dapper appearance and off-course antics helped to create huge public interest in the sport and his assertion that professional golfers should be accorded the same respect as amateurs has influenced the game to this very day. Back then professional golfers were considered to be at the bottom rung of the golfing ladder, especially in Britain. They were not allowed to enjoy the facilities of the clubhouse and were often prohibited from entering it through the front door. When he arrived for the 1920 Open Championship at Deal, Hagen hired a Daimler and a chauffeur, parked it outside the clubhouse front door and changed inside the car. As Gene Sarazen said, 'All the professionals... today should say a silent thanks to Walter each time they stretch a cheque between their fingers. It was Walter who made professional golf what it is.'

Hagen was also the first golfer to realize the commercial opportunities of product endorsement, indeed he was paid $500 per year for every club he carried. At the height of his popularity he charged considerable appearance fees for exhibition matches, and as a professional at his base in Florida he charged $40 per session. In fact, he became the first golfer to earn and spend a million dollars. And spend he did. While in London, he hired a Rolls-Royce and stayed at the Savoy hotel at a cost of £10,000, the equivalent of a working man's lifetime wage!

Hagen also popularized colourful clothing on the golf course. Just imagine the sight of this American turning up to play the Open in colourful plus fours, tank top and two-tone shoes while the rest of the field

Below: Hagen playing in the Ryder Cup in 1933.
Opposite page: Gene Sarazen with Hagen.

THE MAJORS

Majors:	11
US Open:	1914, 1919
The Open:	1922, 1924 1928, 1929
US PGA	1921, 1924 1925, 1926 1927

were wearing sporting clothes with all the style that brown and grey can afford.

In addition to all this, Walter Hagen was a fine golfer, winning four consecutive US PGA Championships, four British Opens and two US Opens. He captained and played in five Ryder Cup encounters and was non-playing captain in 1937.

Hagen's place in the Hall of Fame is deserved not only because of these achievements but because he brought to the game a sense of sport and style.

THE MAJORS

Majors:	9
Masters:	1951, 1953
US Open:	1948, 1950, 1951, 1953
The Open:	1953
US PGA:	1946, 1948

BEN HOGAN

1912 – 1997

Hogan was born in Dublin, Texas, the son of a village blacksmith. He entered the golfing world as a caddy and gradually began to perfect his own game through practice and determination. By 1940, he had ended the year as the leading money winner, and having been interrupted by World War II, he continued to develop his career. By 1949, Hogan had secured three major titles, the US PGA in 1946 and in 1948 and the first US Open in the same year. An intense player with a concentrated game, the 'Iceman' was admired rather than loved by the crowd.

But Hogan's life was as dramatic as it was successful. In early 1949 a near-fatal car accident changed the course of his career. He and his wife Valerie had been driving to their home in Fort Worth, Texas when a Greyhound bus came out of the fog and hit his car head on. Hogan had leaned across the passenger seat to protect his wife and in doing so saved not only her life but his own too; the impact crushed the driver's side of the car. His life had been saved but it was feared he would never walk again, let alone play golf. Showing the same determination that had been apparent earlier on, he worked to prove the doctors wrong.

Opposite page & Below: Hogan drives off at Wentworth during the Canada Cup in 1956.

Within a year Hogan was playing again, although initially traversing the fairways in a motor scooter. He would never manage another US PGA; playing two rounds in one day was too much for his shattered body, but Hogan did win three more US Opens, one British Open and two US Masters tournaments. Significantly, he achieved as near to a grand slam as was possible, securing all three of the above majors in 1953, a feat only since equalled by Tiger Woods. Hogan's incredible return to the game won him the hearts of the public on both sides of the Atlantic. Indeed, his return from the Open was greeted by a tickertape parade through the streets of New York, the first for a golfer since Bobby Jones in 1930. Such an incredible story was accorded Hollywood treatment and the actor Glenn Ford played Hogan in the film of his life, *Follow the Sun.*

TONY JACKLIN

1944 -

Tony Jacklin will always be fondly remembered as the player who lifted British golf out of the doldrums. When Jacklin first started playing in the early 60s the sport was dominated by the Americans: the US Open hadn't been won by a Briton since Ted Ray in 1920, the Ryder Cup had lost its competitive edge with each predictable American victory and the PGA European Tour was still in its infancy. Tony Jacklin changed all that.

Jacklin came from very different roots to Henry Cotton, the last British hero. The son of a lorry driver, he began working as a steelworker in Scunthorpe whilst pursuing golf in his spare time. His natural talent ensured that he picked up a number of amateur titles before turning professional in 1962. In 1968 Jacklin won the Jacksonville Open, the first indication that he could take on the Americans on their own soil. His star had begun to rise. The following year he won the Open at Royal Lytham and St. Annes, the first Briton to do so for 18 years. Then, in 1970, came his most significant victory. Jacklin stole the US Open at Hazeltine, winning by seven strokes, the biggest margin since 1921 and the first British player to do so to date.

Jacklin was a superb player, but his game was badly affected by psychological pressure. Despite a brilliant first day in the 1970 Open, he lost his nerve after weather called a halt to the proceedings, and subsequently lost his title. In 1972, Lee Trevino infamously snatched a win from Jacklin with a fluke shot that destroyed Jacklin's composure. He would never win a major again.

But Jacklin's fortunes were not completely lost. He was captain of the European Ryder Cup team three times, including the winning sides of 1985 and 1987. The 1985 victory at the Belfry was the first for 48 years and Jacklin was an inspirational captain. Then, two years later, the European team won an emotional victory on American soil for the first time. The captain of that US team? Lee Trevino.

British golf is indebted to Tony Jacklin not only for his successes on the fairway, but also for his contribution to the growth of the European tour. He fully deserves his place in the Hall of Fame.

Below: When Jacklin won the Open trophy in 1969, he was the first Briton to do so for 18 years.

THE MAJORS

Majors:	2
US Open:	1970
The Open:	1969

BOBBY JONES

1902 – 1971

Robert Tyre Jones has taken on almost legendary status for his contribution to the game. He was a true amateur for whom golf came third, after his family and his career. Yet by the time he reached 28 years of age, he had won every title available to him and no amateur since has achieved as much.

Born in Atlanta, Georgia, Bobby Jones was not expected to survive infancy due to a digestive ailment, but he did and took up golf as a hobby aged five. At 11 he shot 80 on a 6,500 yard course, and aged 14 he entered his first Amateur at Merion. Jones never gave up his amateur status, indeed he was a fierce supporter it, earning his money from working in his own legal practice. He confined his golf to competing in major championships, and as he won each of those he was also busy studying for degrees in law, English literature and mechanical engineering at three different Universities. His golfing achievements are well known. He won his first US Open in 1923 and in the following eight years he won thirteen national championships. In 1930, Jones won the original Grand Slam, an unrepeatable performance in which he took the Amateur and Open championships on both sides of the Atlantic.

Opposite page & below: By the time Jones was 28 he had won every major title available to him.

While Jones was a natural talent he was not a natural superstar. He suffered acutely from nerves and could not bear large crowds. Unfortunately, thousands would turn out to watch the famous Bobby play. During the 1930 US Amateur at Merion, the final leg of his Grand Slam, Jones momentarily lost his form as a result of his claustrophobia, but overcoming his nerves, he went on to crush his opponent. Even after his retirement Jones attracted large crowds. In 1936, whilst holidaying in Scotland, he played a sentimental round at St Andrews with friends. Word got out that Bobby Jones was back and by the time he reached the first tee, almost 2,000 spectators had gathered to follow him around the course, with the crowd growing as the round progressed.

THE MAJORS

Majors:	7
US Open:	1923, 1926, 1929, 1930 (all as amateur)
The Open:	1926, 1927, 1930 (all as amateur)

Jones retired from golf early, at the age of 28, with no major titles left to win. His presence in the game had not, however, ended. His retirement dream was to build his own private course in Atlanta, and to invite his friends to play away from the crowds. The Augusta National Golf Club resulted, and with it the US Masters Tournament, hosted by its founder.

Certainly the greatest amateur in the history of the game, Jones was a much loved and admired sportsman whose place in the hall of fame is without question.

BOBBY LOCKE

1917 - 1987

Born in Germiston, South Africa, Bobby Locke dominated golf in his home country winning its Open Championship nine times between 1935 and 1956. To the South Africans he became known as the 'golfing robot' for his concentrated and unemotional play, while the Americans, with whom he had a strained relationship, dubbed him, 'Old Muffin Face'. Locke's real name was Arthur d'Arcy Locke, but he was known as Bobby after his hero, Bobby Jones.

Locke began playing in Britain in 1936 when his employers sent him to London, and his fame grew when he won the Harry Vardon Cup in that same year. His career was interrupted by the Second World War, during which he served with distinction in the South African Air Force. He then went to the United States where, much to the chagrin of the Americans, he became a regular winner on the Tour circuit, taking an impressive eleven Tour titles in three years. He even managed to win four tournaments during a five week period in 1947. Locke eventually won the

Below & Opposite page: Bobby Locke at the height of his career in 1950.

Open in 1949 and decided to stay in Britain, further enraging the US PGA who consequently barred him from the US Tour. Even after the ban was lifted, Locke would never play in the United States again.

Locke was an individual figure; he almost always wore plus fours with his trademark white cap and his style of play made him stand out. He played with a pronounced hook that infuriated many yet was a deliberate and controlled shot that gave him more run on the ball. On the green, he was a skilful putter, although his putting 'style' was in fact a hook. However he thought it a bad day if he took more than 28 putts on a round!

Bobby Locke's golfing career was ended abruptly following a serious car accident in 1959. However he had accumulated over 80 titles around the world and was eventually honoured with membership of the R&A in 1976.

THE MAJORS

Majors: 4

The Open: 1949, 1950,
            1952, 1957

THE MAJORS

Majors: 2

US Open: 1973

The Open: 1976

JOHNNY MILLER

1947 –

ohnny Miller now enjoys a career as a sharp and insightful commentator for NBC. However he was once considered a highly talented golfer, with two Major victories to his credit, the 1973 US Open and the 1976 Open.

The handsome, golden-haired Californian was born in 1947 and turned professional in 1969. In 1964, Miller had watched as Tony Lema, another San Franciscan won the Open and he dreamed of doing the same. Then in 1966, he went to the US Open in San Francisco intending to caddie, but instead played and finished eighth. His game was to peak in the seventies. His victory in the US Open at Oakmont was impressive and he nearly took a Masters title from Jack Nicklaus in 1975, losing out by only one stroke. Then, in 1976 at Royal Birkdale, he beat both Jack Nicklaus and Seve Ballesteros, two of the game's indisputable masters, into second place at the Open to achieve that long held dream.

Below: Miller poses for photographers in London in October 1974, with a selection of clubs.

Johnny Miller seemed unable to hold onto that form. A devout Mormon, he had six children to support and recognized that money was not the only means by which he could do this. Once he had achieved financial stability he opted to spend far more time with his family and lost the desire to commit himself to his sport.

Miller's role as a family man even impacted on his game. In the US PGA Championship of 1976, he was penalized for carrying an extra club, breaking one of golf's many rules. The offending club was an 18-inch plastic one, used two days earlier by his young son and dropped into the bottom of his tournament bag by mistake.

OLD TOM MORRIS

1821 – 1908

Born in St Andrews, Scotland, Tom Morris's legacy to the game reaches further than simply his achievements on the course. He was a course designer, an equipment manufacturer and Custodian to the Links at the R&A Club, St. Andrews.

Morris lived in an age when the game was the preserve of the wealthy, due to the cost of hand-crafted clubs and balls. Apprenticed to the ball maker Allan Robertson, in a business that overlooked the 18th green at St Andrews, Morris was surrounded golf and it is no surprise that he took up the sport himself. Together with Robertson, he formed a golfing partnership that was invincible; they remained undefeated until Robertson's death in 1859.

Despite their falling out over Morris's introduction of the gutta percha ball which rendered Robertson's 'featherie' obsolete, Morris still took part in the championship which was introduced at Prestwick to honour Robertson's memory, the very first British Open. Although the favourite to win, Morris came second to Willie Park but he would get other opportunities to play in the competition. Tom Morris went on to win the Open four times, beginning in 1861, the year after he lost it to Park. He won the following year and claimed the third Open by 13 strokes, the widest margin of victory at a major championship, and a record that stood for 138 years until Tiger Woods broke it at the US Open in 2000. Morris played in every Open until 1896 when he was 75.

In 1865, Morris returned to St Andrews as groundskeeper, taking care of the Old Course for the R&A for an annual fee of £50. He was fiercely protective of the course, regarding it almost as his own property. In one incident he was publicly reprimanded for prematurely closing it as he believed it needed 'a rest'.

Old Tom Morris outlived his wife and all of his children, and at his funeral in 1908, great crowds turned out to honour him. His service to the game is still remembered and the R&A has hung his portrait on permanent display in the clubhouse.

Opposite Page: Old Tom Morris (left) watches as Kirkaldy tees off during a foursome match for £100-a-side at St Andrews. The other two golfers in the foursome were Archie Simpson and Sandy Herd.

YOUNG TOM MORRIS

1851 – 1875

I n a life and career cut tragically short, Young Tom Morris, son of the famous Old Tom, made a deep impression on the game. He won the Open four times consecutively and it was as a result of his first three wins that the organizers took the decision to change the format of the competition, taking a year off to do so. Had Tom not died at the tender age of 24, who knows what other impact he might have had on British golf.

Young Tom was considered to be a far more skilled player than his father. He grew up at Prestwick where Old Tom was groundskeeper, and played in his first tournament aged 13, beating leading professionals. He succeeded his father in winning the Open for the first time in 1868, when he was aged just 17. Old Tom had been the oldest winner of the competition, Young Tom became the youngest. His talent was impressive in an age when courses and equipment were far less refined than today. He won the first Open by two strokes and the next by three. In his third Open, he played 36 holes in just 149 strokes, 12 shots ahead of the next players. After this third victory Young Tom was awarded the winners belt outright. There was no tournament the following year while the organizers raised money for the next trophy, the claret jug that is still played for today. When the competition was revived, Young Tom's was the first name to be inscribed on it.

Young Tom's dominance came to a premature end in 1875. He was competing

in a challenge match at North Berwick when news came of his wife's death in childbirth, together with his newborn son. Broken hearted, Tom died just a few months later. Between them, Young Tom Morris and his father won the Open eight times in twelve years, a dynastic record that is highly unlikely to be broken.

BYRON NELSON

1912 -

Born in Fort Worth, Texas, Byron Nelson clocked up an impressive 18 wins during seven months in 1945, which included 11 consecutive victories. Add to this his feat of winning one US Open, two US Masters and three US PGA tournaments and it is easy to see why Nelson is still considered one of the great players in American history.

Nelson's early career ran parallel to that of Ben Hogan; they were born in the same district, in the same year and they both caddied at the same club. However, Nelson's career took off sooner than Hogan's, and he turned professional in 1932. Within five years, Nelson had won his first major, the US Masters and had been selected for that year's Ryder Cup squad.

However, just as with Hogan and Snead, the war interrupted Nelson's golfing and although he won titles during the war years, many of his contemporaries had been sent off to fight, something which undoubtedly casts a shadow over his achievements.

As a haemophiliac, Nelson was forced to stay at home and was able to work on his technique. This included adopting steel shafted clubs instead of wooden ones, resulting in greater distance and consistency. Although he had some success directly after the war, Ben Hogan's career had begun to take off and at the age of 34, Nelson retired from the game. He did occasionally play again and win, but he had effectively ended his professional career on a high note.

Below: Five years after Nelson had officially retired, he still continued to play and win.

Nelson retired to live on the Texas ranch that he had paid for with his earnings as one of the games top money winners, and set up the tournament which still carries his name. He had played in 113 tournaments in the 1940s and had finished in the top ten of every one of them. His 54 wins on the US tour places him in the top five winners, behind Snead, Nicklaus, Hogan and Palmer.

THE MAJORS

Majors:	5
Masters:	1937, 1942
US Open:	1939
US PGA:	1940, 1945

THE MAJORS

Majors:	18
Masters:	1963, 1965, 1966, 1972, 1975, 1986
US Open:	1962, 1967, 1972, 1980
The Open:	1966, 1970, 1988
US PGA:	1963, 1971, 1973, 1975, 1980

JACK NICKLAUS

1940 –

J ack Nicklaus began his incredible career with the nickname 'Ohio Fats,' awarded to him by Arnold Palmer fans who were annoyed by his victory over the waning star at the 1962 US Open. Twenty-four years later, 'The Golden Bear', as he is now known, picked up his eighteenth Major, by winning his sixth US Masters title. Nicklaus echoed Bobby Jones when he stated that 'victories in the major championships are the only ones that really matter' and therefore by his own estimation as well as that of his fellow golfers, Jack Nicklaus is the greatest golfer of the modern era, winning more major championships than anyone else in history.

Nicklaus took up the game at the age of 10 and by the time he was 19 he had won his first US Amateur Championship. He won the Amateur again (bringing his major tournament record up to 20) before turning professional in 1961. His first foray into the US Open landed him the runner-up position, second to Arnold Palmer, who he would later beat. When Nicklaus won his final major at Augusta, he was 46 years old and widely considered to be over the hill, not least by himself. His victory there was all the more sweet because it was so unexpected. It also sealed the assertion that Nicklaus was the best golfer of all time - he had been winning tournaments for a quarter of a century.

Opposite page: It was in 1969 that Nicklaus first appeared in the Ryder Cup.

Nicklaus's ability rested not only on his incredible power and grace – he could hit a ball further and higher than anyone else – but also on his immense powers of concentration when under great pressure. During that first US Open tournament, when Nicklaus had tied Palmer, he was an unpopular opponent for the partisan crowd who took to applauding all of his mistakes.

Now of course, Nicklaus is one of the world's most popular sportsmen. He has won every honour that it is possible to win in golf and is an inspiration for young golfers everywhere. Just as Bobby Jones was Nicklaus's hero, so Jack has influenced the game of young legends such as Tiger Woods.

GREG NORMAN

1955 -

Born in Mount Isa, Queensland, Norman is Australia's most successful golfer, boasting a total of 77 victories worldwide, which includes two British Open championships. Unfortunately however, he is rather better known as the golfer who has lost a play-off at all four of the majors, a runners-up Grand Slam!

Norman first took to golf aged 17; his introduction to the game had been as caddy for his mother. He was a naturally gifted player, with a particularly long and accurate drive. His talent was immediately apparent; he won on only his fourth tournament appearance in his homeland and turned professional in 1976. The following year, Norman arrived in Europe and won the Martini International, finishing twentieth in the Order of Merit. From this victory, Norman went on to claim many more and with victory on the course came money.

1986, when he first won the Open, was a particularly impressive financial year. For winning the European Open at Sunningdale he received prize money of £35,000 plus a bonus cheque of £50,000 for winning both tournaments. Victory in the Dunhill Cup secured £69,000 and the World Matchplay Championship brought in £50,000. Adding these sums to the original Open Championship cheque of £70,000 ensured

Below & Opposite page: Norman has always been noted for his long hitting.

that Norman passed the $1 million mark for that season. He had already headed the money list in 1982 and he certainly is proof that professional golf at the top level can be a lucrative game!

However, all those dollars in the bank doesn't change the fact that he only has two Major Championships to his name, the Open in 1986 and 1993. Norman has definitely been unlucky in his share of defeats. He has finished second in three different US Masters play-offs, while in 1986, he had led in the other three Majors only to finish runner-up. At the PGA championship,

THE MAJORS

Majors:	2
The Open:	1986, 1993

Norman had led with a four stroke lead before Bob Tway stole the title from him at the final hole. Even more dramatically, in the 1996 Masters, Norman lost to Nick Faldo after holding a six-shot last round lead.

Ultimately, Greg Norman has proved to be a superstar at the game, and he is fully entitled to enjoy the profits of his golfing labours as the head of a huge business empire.

THE MAJORS

Majors:	7
Masters:	1958, 1960, 1962, 1964
US Open:	1960
The Open:	1961, 1962

ARNOLD PALMER

1929 -

Arnold Palmer was the first great golfing media star, the player who brought golf to the attention of the American public with his powerful and thrilling game. He turned professional in 1954 and his rise on the circuit coincided with the boom in television audiences. In one sense golf had been a minority sport before 'Arnie' hit the screens; during the sixties, with corporate support, the game was to germinate into the well-financed industry that we have today. A hugely popular and charismatic player, Palmer travelled with an entourage of devoted fans, known as 'Arnie's Army' who would excitedly cheer on their hero, and Palmer rarely let them down, even when he lost. He would make birdies from impossible positions, swing huge drives off the tee and snatch victory from the jaws of defeat.

In a career that has spanned almost fifty years the famous golfer amassed over 90 championships. Sixty-one of those victories came on the US PGA Tour. Palmer picked up one US Open title in 1960 and won the US Masters four times. However, he can also be credited with breathing new life into the British Open, which he won twice in 1961 and 1962. During the 50s many of the best American players overlooked the Open, preferring to concentrate on the US PGA tour. Palmer, however, enjoyed the links game and with him came not only his entourage and therefore publicity, but also many of his compatriots.

Opposite page: Palmer puts in a bit of practice before the Open in July 1961.

Palmer was eventually eclipsed by the young Jack Nicklaus and it is easy to see why the young, chubby Nicklaus found it initially difficult to win over American crowds; Palmer was a handsome and powerful presence. He inherited his incredible upper body strength from his father, a professional golfer himself, who would apparently complete ten single-handed pull-ups with each arm as exercise.

A golfing superstar, Palmer was the first player to amass earnings of $1million. His impact on the game has been indisputable; he brought golf to the public as a form of entertainment, and for this he deserves his place as one of the game's greatest stars.

GARY PLAYER

1935 -

During the 1960s three men were to dominate the game, the 'Big Three' consisted of the Americans, Jack Nicklaus and Arnold Palmer and a talented South African golfer, Gary Player. While the other two always had an advantage of playing to a home crowd, Player's success in nine Majors was all the greater for their being won on foreign soil. Gary Player was indeed a very special sportsman, collecting 167 titles in a career that has lasted for half a century.

Although classed as one of the 'Big Three', Player is, in stature, a small man. Indeed his height, 5'7", and relatively light weight led some of his early contemporaries to believe that golf was the wrong game for him. However, by following a strenuous physical exercise regime and maintaining an incredibly confident approach, he proved his critics wrong. Known as the 'Black Knight' for his trademark monochrome clothes, Player believed that the black absorbed sunlight therefore making him stronger. Even now he is recognized for his incredible strength and fitness; legend has it he is strong enough to do 100 press ups with a full suitcase on his back!

Below & Opposite page: Despite his alleged 'poor swing' Player has had a very successful career.

Player arrived in Britain at the age of 19 from a South Africa that was in the grip of apartheid and a year later, in 1956, he won his first tournament, the Dunlop Masters. That win took him to the United States where he studied Ben Hogan and just two years later, in 1959, he won his first Major title. Since then he has accumulated among others: 7 Australian Opens, 13 South African Opens and five World Matchplay titles. One of his greatest personal achievements was to become the third person to win the Grand Slam of all four Major titles; only four other players have achieved this feat.

Like many South African sportsmen and women, Player encountered his share of hostility during the height of his career. Yet he

THE MAJORS

Majors:	9
Masters:	1961, 1974, 1978
US Open:	1965
The Open:	1959, 1968, 1974
US PGA:	1962, 1972

never left his homeland fully, and many of those who protested against him were not to know that as his wealth increased so did his contributions to the welfare and education of young black children.

Unlike many foreign players, he never settled in the US and is well known for the amount of travelling he has done in order to compete. He is golf's most travelled sportsman, clocking up an estimated 12 million air miles to date.

THE MAJORS

Majors:	7
Masters:	1935
US Open:	1922, 1932
The Open:	1932
US PGA:	1922, 1923, 1933

GENE SARAZEN

1902 - 1999

At Augusta in 1935, Gene Sarazen played 'the shot heard around the world'. It was the second US Masters tournament and the first that Sarazen had played in. He was three down with four to play when he hit his second at the 15th across the lake and into the hole for an albatross. It was generally considered to be the shot that put the Masters tournament on the map and it certainly helped him to secure victory. With that win, Sarazen became the first of only five players to have won all four Grand Slam trophies during their career.

He was a true legend, enjoying one of the longest and most successful golfing careers in history. Sarazen won a total of nine Major tournaments. At the tender age of twenty, he won both the US Open and the US PGA, the first man to win both titles in the same year. He took the US PGA the following year and again in 1933. His second US Open title came in 1932, the same year that he won the British Open at Prince's. Sarazen continued to add to his legendary status in 1973 in the Open at Troon, when aged 71 he holed-in-one at the famous short eighth hole, the 'Postage Stamp'.

Below & Opposite page: Sarazen started his career as a caddy, but had won three major events by the age of 21.

Yet Sarazen's career may never have happened had it not been for ill-health during childhood. As the son of a carpenter in New York, Eugenio Saraceni was expected to follow the family business; however due to the dust in the wood shop doctors advised the teenage Gene to work outdoors. Sarazen took a job as an assistant at a local golf course, eventually becoming a caddy. Encouraged by the professionals there he entered his first tournament, the 1920 US Open as a player. Although he finished well down the order, he was not to be discouraged and of course, the rest of the rags-to-riches story is history.

A friend and contemporary of Walter Hagen and Bobby Jones, Sarazen belongs to that golden age of golf before the War, when firsts were made and records were set. He remained a public figure, as honourary starter at the Masters until his death at the age of 97.

SAM SNEAD

1912 - 2002

'S lammin' Sam' Snead was admired for his natural talent; his flowing swing was coveted by his contemporaries and, as one rival put it, 'Sam just walked up to the ball and poured honey all over it.' Born in Hot Springs, Virginia, Snead was often considered to be a hillbilly player who had fashioned his first club from the branch of a swamp maple tree and who played barefoot. In reality he was a talented and athletic boy who could just have easily had a career in American football were it not for a back injury. Growing up during the Depression, Snead learned to play by watching his older brother hit massive drives across the fields of the family farm. He eventually became a caddy at Hot Springs and then an assistant at Greenbrier, his home course. Revered for his effortless skill, it was once said that 'watching Sam Snead practise hitting golf balls is like watching a fish practise swimming.' He was the first great golfer regularly to drive 300 yards and more and, in 1984, could still play par golf and make money on the US Senior Tour at the age of 72.

Below: Snead in action during the Ryder Cup in 1953.

Snead's record is full of impressive victories; he won seven Major titles and a record 82 PGA Tour wins in America in a career that spanned six decades. Yet despite all this, Snead is often remembered as the player who failed to win the US Open. He was a runner-up four times, but his most infamous US Open occurred in 1939 at Philadelphia Country Club. There were no scoreboards on the course, and Snead thought he needed a birdie on the final hole to win, when all he actually needed was a par. Playing aggressively, he hit his drive into the left rough and never recovered, making a triple bogey.

He won three Masters, three US PGA Championships and the 1946 Open at St. Andrews, a course he disliked enough to publicly criticize. Indeed, Snead's disdain for the British Championship meant that he never bothered to compete for it again. He continued to compete for

THE MAJORS

Majors:	7
Masters:	1949, 1952, 1954
The Open:	1946
US PGA:	1942, 1949, 1951

championship titles well into his sixties, and in 1969 he became the youngest player to score below his age, a 66 when he was 67. Snead had also played in seven Ryder Cup tournaments and lost out on captaining the winning side in 1969 when the United States controversially tied with Europe, following Jack Nicklaus's conceded putt to Tony Jacklin.

An American legend, Sam Snead died where he was born, in Hot Springs, aged 89.

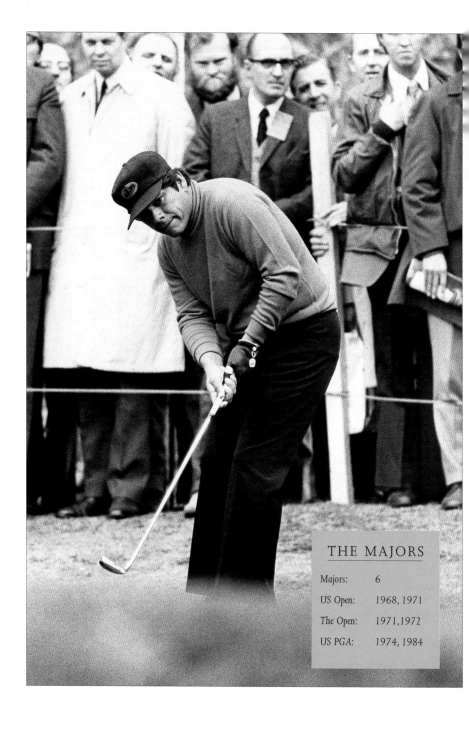

THE MAJORS

Majors:	6
US Open:	1968, 1971
The Open:	1971, 1972
US PGA:	1974, 1984

LEE TREVINO

1939 -

L ee Trevino is one of the great personalities of golf. Known for his wicked sense of humour and sharp wit on the course, Trevino was also a fine player in his heyday. Trevino acquired six Major titles in a career that has continued onto the senior circuit. His first Major victory was in 1968 in the US Open at Oak Hill; his last, despite having been struck by lightening in 1975, was sixteen years later in the 1984 US PGA. Among his many credits, Trevino can count being the winner of the national championships of three different countries during a three week period. He won the US Open, the Canadian Open and the British Open in consecutive weeks during 1971. Only Tiger Woods has come close to achieving the same feat, winning three Opens in succession but not in as many weeks.

Yet Trevino came from the humblest of beginnings. Born in Texas, Lee Buck Trevino was the illegitimate son of an immigrant Mexican gravedigger. His home stood in a hayfield next to the Glen Lakes Country Club and he ventured onto the course to look for lost golf balls to sell. He later became a sergeant in the Marines where he was given time and encouragement with his golf and he turned professional soon after his discharge in 1961. It would be several years before Trevino started earning serious money from his sport. As a teaching pro in Texas he was extremely poor, living with his wife in a trailer on the edge of the course. It was his wife who encouraged him to enter the 1966 US Open in San Francisco, where he finished 54th out of 64 players. In the 1967 US Open he came fifth. Then, in 1968, victory as Trevino knocked Jack Nicklaus into second place. By 1970, Trevino had topped the money list and in 1971, he was named player of the year.

Trevino was as famous for his humour and streetwise patter as he was for his game. On one memorable occasion he produced a rubber snake from the grass at the first tee of the 1971 Open play-off, dancing around with it draped over his clubhead. High jinx like this earned him the nickname 'Merry Mex' although later it would become 'Supermex'. A truly popular player, Trevino brought back some of the fun first introduced to the game by Walter Hagen.

Below: Trevino displays his score sheet after winning the Open in 1971.

HARRY VARDON

1870 - 1937

A t the turn of the last century, three men dominated the game, known as the 'Great Triumvirate' they were the original 'Big Three': James Braid, J.H. Taylor and the most impressive of them all, Harry Vardon. Vardon had a huge impact on the game, he popularized the overlapping grip, still used today and known as the Vardon Grip. He also developed the modern upright swing, a move away from the more fashionable sweeping action of the time. His accuracy and low scoring were legendary. By all accounts he could strike a ball so cleanly that he never took a divot. His scoring is still commemorated with the Vardon Trophy, awarded annually to the European Tour player with the lowest stroke average.

At his peak, Vardon was almost invincible, and remains the only player to date to have won the Open Championship six times. Vardon's great rival was his colleague, J. H. Taylor whom he beat in his first Open in 1896 and again in his last in 1914. He also achieved what was, at the time, a fantastic victory at the US Open in 1903. Very few British players crossed the Atlantic for the tournament which was, inevitably, dominated by American golfers. Yet there were very few tournaments open for professionals at the time and so Vardon and Taylor made the trip in order to tour the United States for a year. When they entered the competition no one else was to get a look in, Vardon beat Taylor into second place.

Below & Opposite page: Vardon's style of play was cited as a model for aspiring young golfers.

It was at this point in his career that Vardon was struck down with tuberculosis, an illness from which he never really recovered. Although he continued to play, and to win, he was never quite the same again and blamed the illness for his difficulties with a putter. Incredibly, Vardon's TB first surfaced during the Open Championship at Prestwick. Despite feeling seriously ill and coughing up blood, he pushed on to win the game, beating his brother, Tom, by six strokes.

Certainly the one of the best British golfers in history, Harry Vardon was instrumental in popularizing the sport at the beginning of the twentieth century.

THE MAJORS

Majors:	7
US Open:	1900
The Open:	1896, 1898 1899, 1903 1911, 1914

TOM WATSON

1949 -

om Watson came close to equalling Harry Vardon's long held record of six Open Championship victories, when in 1984 he lost out to Seve Ballesteros. He had already matched the accomplishments of J.H.Taylor, James Braid and Peter Thompson by winning five Opens between 1975 and 1983, the first American to do so. In total Tom Watson achieved 8 Major victories during his career; he won the US Open in 1982 and the US Masters in 1977 and 1981. Unfortunately the US PGA also eluded him, denying him the title of Grand Slam winner; however his successful record and his position as leading money winner for four consecutive years are testament to his greatness as a golfer.

Yet it was not always so. Watson had come to golf later in life than many, he had begun playing while at University studying Psychology; he turned professional in 1971 following his graduation and played a steady, reliable game. However, once Watson began to come close to winning tournaments, he also began to lose his nerve, throwing victories away. He was cruelly labelled a 'choker' and it wasn't until the great Byron Nelson took

Opposite page: Watson won both the Masters and the Open in 1977.

Watson under his wing that he finally got a grip on his game and the titles began to roll in. British fans never really understood the 'choker' label. In the Open at Carnoustie in 1975, Watson played Jock Newton in a tense play-off and showed no signs of choking. Nor did he do so in the Ryder Cup two years later.

Watson's love of the British game was to benefit British golf. Many Americans disliked the unpredictability of the links courses, but Watson loved them. He brought with him other American players, keen to succeed at the Open, and was involved in one of the most hotly contested and thrilling matches, in 1977 against Jack Nicklaus. The 'duel in the sun' as it became known ended a week of high drama at Turnberry, culminating in a head-to-head competition with Watson

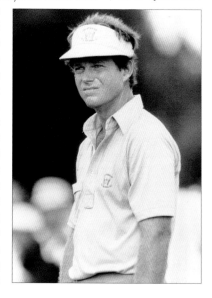

THE MAJORS

Majors:	8
Masters:	1977. 1981
US Open:	1982
The Open:	1975, 1977, 1980, 1982, 1983

needing to birdie for victory. His defeat of Nicklaus was impressive, but it did little to win favour with Nicklaus's fans, just as Jack's defeat of Arnold Palmer had made him unpopular.

Watson retired from the game in 1991. His victories were earned through perseverance and determination and while he has perhaps not earned the popularity that he deserves, his place in golf's history is assured.

TIGER WOODS

1975 -

I f there is one player who has made golf a multi-million pound industry and one of the most popular sports on the planet then it is Tiger Woods. The meteoric rise of this young American is breathtaking. As the son of an African-American father and a Thai mother, he has opened the game up to young people of all backgrounds, fuelling an interest in the sport worldwide.

Woods turned professional in 1996; however his amateur career was record breaking in itself. In 1994, at the age of 19, he became the youngest ever winner of the US Amateur and, by winning it twice more, he become the first player to win it three years in succession. As a professional, Woods continued to collect titles and to break records. He won his first Masters in 1996, winning with a record 270 total, breaking the 72-hole record. He has, in the seven years since he turned professional, won eight Major titles, including holding all four Majors consecutively, the US PGA, US Open and British Open in 2000 and the US Masters in 2001, and is only the fifth player in history to have won all four Majors. Add to this the fact that Woods is the youngest player to have won 20 events on the US Tour and that he tops the world rankings by a huge margin and there is plenty of evidence for his popularity.

Below & Opposite page: Young American player Woods has taken the world of golf by storm since 1995.

Eldrick Woods was born in California and his father gave his son the nickname 'Tiger', after a soldier and friend from his days in the U.S. Army. Legend has it that even as a baby, Tiger was learning to swing, watching his father play as he lay in his crib. At the age of two he appeared on the Bob Hope Show, playing shots and at five he had succeeded in shooting 48 for 9!

His career has, in reality, only just begun; many of golf's greatest players continue in their game for several decades, and with this in mind it is surely possible that the determined Tiger will beat Jack Nicklaus's record 18 Majors.

THE MAJORS

Majors:	8
Masters:	1997, 2001, 2002
US Open:	2000, 2002
The Open:	2000
US PGA:	1999, 2000

THE CONTENDERS

Today there are hundreds of players competing for the major honours. Here are just some of the players who are in contention for the game's rich prizes at the start of the 21st century. It remains to be seen who will earn their place amongst the golfing elite.

FRED COUPLES

1959 –

Born in Washington, Couples became one of America's key players of the late eighties and nineties and as such one of their most popular stars, winning 14 times on the US tour. He has participated in the Presidents Cup three times and five Ryder Cup matches. Despite being plagued by back problems, he is capable of both skilful golf and almost amateurish shenanigans. He won the US Masters in 1992, his only major tournament victory. He was also twice voted PGA Tour Player of the Year in 1991 and 1992.

His powerful swing and huge drives have earned Couples the nickname 'Boom Boom' and' whilst he may not have always benefited from his technique' he has remained one of America's favourite players.

THE MAJORS

Majors:	1
Masters:	1992

ERNIE ELS

1969 –

A t a towering six-foot-three, it is no surprise that this strapping South African has a swing big enough to put fear into his opponents; however, it is the grace with which he plays that has earned him the nickname 'The Big Easy'. Born in Johannesburg, Els could have chosen either rugby union or cricket but instead turned professional golfer, aged 20. Just five years later he became the first South African since Gary Player to sweep through the South African Open, PGA and Masters in one year. He went on to equal Player's record of three successive South African Opens.

Els has proved himself as dangerous abroad as he is at home. He won the US Open twice, first in 1994, when almost unknown to the American crowd, and again in 1997. Along with team mates Retief Goosen and David Frost, he won the Dunhill Cup in 1998. He eventually succeeded in winning the British Open at Muirfield in 2002, thwarting Tiger Woods's hopes of taking all four Majors in the same year.

THE MAJORS

Majors:	3
US Open:	1994, 1997
The Open:	2002

SERGIO GARCIA

1980 –

Sergio Garcia made a deep impression on the game whilst playing as an amateur. When he turned professional in 1999 he was ready to assume his place as one of golf's new leading lights. In that first year, Garcia won two European Tour events, played in Europe's Ryder Cup team, under the captaincy of Mark James, and was runner up to Tiger Woods in the US PGA.

An extravagant and extrovert player, Garcia looks set to succeed Ballesteros and Olazabal as one of Spain's greatest golfers. He helped his country to capture the Dunhill Cup in 1999 and had an impressive impact on the Ryder Cup team of 2002. He has now begun collecting US tour trophies. It remains to be seen whether 'El Nino' can maintain his position at the top of the world rankings and begin collecting major titles.

BERNHARD LANGER

1957 –

Bernhard Langer's greatest triumph could be said to be his conquest of that putting affliction known as 'the yips'. A golfer's nightmare, Langer has suffered from the 'yips' throughout his career and has tried different remedies to defeat the problem. Changing putters has been one cure, as has changing grips, alternating between a conventional grip for longer putts and a left below right grip for the short ones. He has even evolved the left below right with the right hand clamping the upper handle to the left forearm! In 1980, Langer famously bought a second-hand lady's putter, an Acushnet Bull's Eye for £5 and customized it to suit his game.

However, despite this affliction, Langer has produced some impressive golf, and has earned his green blazer twice, winning the US Masters in 1985 and 1993. He has never won the Open, coming second twice, but has taken the British PGA Championship and five German Opens.

A highly respected player, Langer has popularized the game in his native Germany and has played in the Ryder Cup nine times, proving to be an important influence on European golf.

THE MAJORS

Majors:	2
Masters:	1985, 1993

DAVIS LOVE III

1964 –

Born in Charlotte, North Carolina, Davis Love has a fine swing and a skillful touch on the green, possibly a legacy from his father, one of America's most respected golf teachers, who was tragically killed in a plane crash in 1988. Love's father was considered one of the best swing teachers in the game and consequently Love is one of the longest hitters in the game. He honoured his father's teachings in his book, *Every Shot I Take*.

Although he is a highly regarded player and a stalwart of the US Ryder Cup team in recent years, Love has only one major to his name: he won the US PGA at Winged Foot in 1997, beating Justin Leonard by five shots. He has taken the runner-up position in the 1996 US Open and in the 1999 Masters, so perhaps more victories are in the offing.

Below: Love greets Tiger Woods.

THE MAJORS

Majors: 1

US PGA: 1997

PHIL MICKELSON

1970 –

A right-handed Californian who plays left-handed golf, Phil Mickelson is yet to win a Major tournament, though is generally expected to do so. Mickelson claims to have started playing golf when he was just 18-months-old, which possibly explains his position one of the best-ever left-handed players in the game. His 65 at the 1996 US Masters is the best score by a left-hander in that competition.

He was a highly successful amateur, winning competitions including the Tuscan Open on the US PGA Tour. He turned professional in 1992, winning nineteen tournaments to date. He is one of only three players to win the NCAA Championship and the US Amateur in the same year, keeping company with Jack Nicklaus and Tiger Woods.

Mickleson is considered a key player in the US Ryder Cup teams, having competed in four matches; he has also participated in two Walker Cups and four Presidents Cups.

COLIN MONTGOMERIE

1963 –

Colin Montgomerie has a long list of accolades to his name but he still hasn't achieved his ultimate goal, to win a Major. Indeed he is widely regarded as one of the finest players never to have done so. He has dominated the European Tour and has achieved the remarkable feat of topping the Volvo Order of Merit for seven consecutive years, from 1993 to 1999, beating the previous record holder, Seve Ballesteros.

Introduced to golf by his father, who was secretary at Royal Troon, Montgomerie initially intended to pursue the business and management side of the sport. However, having had a successful amateur career as a junior, he decided to turn professional in 1987, a change in course that he has not lived to regret. He openly admits that his main motivation is to make money from the sport and this may go some way to explaining his lack of a Major title. He plays consistent and accurate golf, taking few risks and always aiming to finish high on the money list of every tournament he plays; he has even earned himself the nickname 'Mr Consistency'. Monty has however, been criticized for not practising or working hard enough at his game. Indeed, he has been accused of not knowing where the driving range is on certain courses!

He has competed in six Ryder Cups for Europe and has proved to be a vital team member. In 2002, Monty scored four-and-a-half out of five, becoming top points scorer and the pillar of strength Europe needed. During a difficult day at Brookline in 1999, he managed to defeat the late Payne Stewart on the final green, in the face of great pressure. Yet Montgomerie has not always enjoyed such calm in the eye of the storm, he can lose his temper when his game isn't going according to plan and sometimes finds it difficult to ignore the taunts of the US galleries and the press. Despite this, Colin Montgomerie is a valued and respected teammate and individual with plenty of well-deserved accolades to his name.

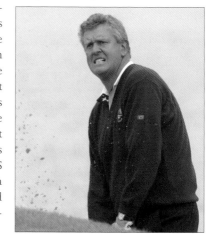

JOSE MARIA OLAZABAL

1966 –

Born in Fuenterrabia, Spain, Olazabal has often unfairly been labelled the 'second Seve', when in fact he is a talented and successful golfer in his own right. He turned professional in 1985 after having enjoyed an impressive amateur career, winning titles such as the British Amateur Championship.

Olazabal's career was almost struck by tragedy, when, in 1995 he was diagnosed with a crippling rheumatoid arthritis in both feet. Housebound and unable to walk, it was feared he would never be able to play golf again. Fortunately, with intense treatment, Olazabal returned to the game after a two year break. Incredibly, he went on to win his second US Masters tournament, beating the luckless Greg Norman in 1999. He had won his first green jacket back in 1994.

He has finished second to Ballesteros on several occasions. However when working in partnership the two together are formidable, as the Americans discovered in the 1987 European Ryder Cup victory at Muirfield Village, Ohio. He has competed with distinction in six Ryder Cups; but it was Olazabal's fate at the 1999 tournament in Brookline to be caught in the middle of an excited and controversial American stampede on the 17th green and not unsurprisingly he missed the putt.

THE MAJORS

Majors: 2

Masters: 1994, 1999

VIJAY SINGH

1963 –

One of the most dedicated players in the game today, Vijay Singh is Fiji's first and only champion golfer. Born in Lautoka, Singh was introduced to the game by his father, an aeroplane engineer and he received no formal training in the game. He is renowned for his thorough practising and famously modelled his swing on that of Tom Weiskopf. He became a club professional in Borneo before eventually making his way to Europe, where he achieved recognition with a victory in the 1992 German Open. Singh had to play for six years in Europe before finding fame in the US, winning the 1998 US PGA Championship and his first Major.

Perhaps best known for his ability to beat other players in tournaments that they desperately want to win, Singh ended Ernie Els' run of three victories in the World Matchplay Championships when he took the title in 1997. More famous was Singh's defeat of Tiger Woods in the 2000 US Masters. Had Woods have won he would have achieved a true Grand Slam, taking all four Majors in one year. It is apt then, that Vijay means 'victory' in Hindi.

THE MAJORS

Majors:	2
Masters:	2000
US PGA:	1998

IAN WOOSNAM

1958 –

Born in England to Welsh parents, Ian Woosnam plays for Wales and, in 1987, he brought the World Cup of Golf to the Principality after beating Scotland's Sandy Lyle and Sam Torrance. A short and stocky player, 'Woosie' is known for his powerful hitting and he credits his great strength with having lifted hay bales when working on his parents' farm!

Woosnam turned professional in 1976, but it was to be some time before he would achieve top-level success. As an aspiring tour star, he was reduced to living in a camper van, until he started to win the National Championships of different countries, beginning with the Swiss Open in 1982. Woosnam soon became the leading money winner and, in the late eighties, his greatest year ended with him heading the European Order of Merit, 1987. It wasn't, however, until 1991 that Woosnam was to win a Major title. At Augusta, he found himself engaged in a battle with Tom Watson and Jose Maria Olazabal, winning the Masters with a nerve-wracking final putt. He is the first Welshman ever to win a Major title.

In 1997, he kept his cool to fend off Faldo and Montgomerie to win the Volvo PGA Championship; the most prestigious event on the PGA European Tour, and in 2001 he won the World Matchplay Tournament for a second time, beating Montgomerie, Westwood and then Harrington in the final. Clearly, Woosnam still has plenty of attack and may yet add to his Majors' total.

THE MAJORS

Majors:	1
Masters:	1991

Woosnam has made an excellent contribution to Europe's Ryder Cup hopes, serving on seven squads, and played alongside Nick Faldo in four winning teams. He was Sam Torrance's vice-captain in 2002 and is widely tipped to be a captain himself, perhaps in 2010 when the tournament comes to Wales.

Perhaps most significantly though, Woosnam no longer needs to travel from tournament to tournament in his camper van; he now enjoys the luxury of his own private jet. Yet despite all his success, he still enjoys a pint with the lads!

CLASSIC COURSES

It is impossible to produce a brief list of courses to please everyone.
Different courses offer different attractions.
The selection here is in some senses arbitrary by necessity;
yet each course is unique or infamous in its own way.
Together they give a brief overview of the challenges,
the history and the legends of the game.

A view across the undulating expanse of the world-famous St Andrews.

THE BELFRY

T he Belfry's two courses, the Brazabon and the Derby have been designed very much along American lines. Both feature a number of water hazards and the 18th hole on the championship Brazabon is dominated by two such challenges.

Opened in 1977, having been transformed from potato fields by Peter Alliss and Dave Thomas, it is for its use as a Ryder Cup venue that the Belfry is best known. It has hosted the event four times with the USA winning only one of the encounters. 1989 was witness to a draw, but in 1985, the European team, captained by Tony Jacklin had enjoyed an emotional triumph as they defeated the USA for the first time in 28 years. In 2002, Sam Torrance captained Europe to another dramatic victory.

CARNOUSTIE

A dramatic and imposing course, Carnoustie's challenges include the best that nature herself has to offer. The course consisted originally of ten holes and was extended to 18 by Old Tom Morris in 1857 then further improved by James Braid in 1926. Nestled on the east coast of Scotland on the Tay Estuary, the course is open to the wild Scottish elements, indeed the wind is the greatest hazard to the golfer. Designed so that each hole faces a different direction, the battle against the wind is always relentless and never repetitive. It features two natural water hazards, Jockie's Burn and the Barry Burn, one of the best-known water hazards in golf. The Barry comes into play on six of the 18 holes and needs to be crossed twice on the 17th, then snakes menacingly across the 18th.

GLENEAGLES

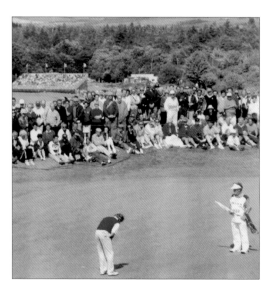

Opened in 1924, the courses at Gleneagles were built in conjunction with the famous hotel. There were initially two - the King's Course and the Queen's Course, both designed by James Braid. Demand was such that the Prince's Course was added in 1974 and the Glendevon in 1980. These latter two were swallowed by the Monarch, the first Jack Nicklaus course in Scotland, which opened in 1993. The holes here are set in beautiful rolling countryside and are very difficult or relatively easy - there is little middle ground.

MUIRFIELD

In 1891, Old Tom Morris designed and laid out a course at Muirfield to be used by the Honourable Company of Edinburgh Golfers. When they moved in, they brought the Open Championship with them and the first Muirfield Open was held a year later. Such a prestigious heritage has ensured that Muirfield is one of the best-known courses in the game.

Muirfield remains a private course; however it has been the home of several Opens, most recently in 2002. It was here that Jack Nicklaus triumphed over Arnold Palmer in his famous 1966 victory, whilst in 1972 Lee Trevino stole the title from Tony Jacklin at the 17th. In 1980, Tom Watson triumphed in impressive style, winning the event with 4 strokes and a total of 271.

Opposite top: John Daly takes a shot on the 12th tee at Muirfield during the Open in 1992.
Opposite below: Head Greenkeeper Colin Irvine (left) and R&A official Alex Dickie watch as Jack Bryce paints the inside of the new hole they have just cut on the 18th at Muirfield.

Above: Peter Higgs at the deadly bunker at the 17th hole at Muirfield.

ROYAL BIRKDALE

One of the courses on the roster of Open venues, Royal Birkdale was founded in 1889 but moved to its present site in 1897. In the early 90s the greens were dug up and replanned, and it is now generally accepted to be one of the best courses on the Championship circuit.

Top: J. Carr on the 12th in the
Walker Cup.
Left: The clubhouse, built in 1931.

ROYAL LYTHAM AND ST ANNES

Having hosted the Open Championship ten times, Royal Lytham and St Annes has been the scene of many a famous victory. The clubhouse holds as souvenir the mashie-iron used by Bobby Jones during his first Open tournament in 1926 and a plaque commemorates the spot where he played his winning shot. In 1969, Tony Jacklin became the first Briton to win the Open for 18 years and in 1996, Tom Lehman was the first American professional to succeed in winning the Championship on the course. Although it is a links, the course is not a traditional seaside one and it is bordered on three sides by dense urban development, and on the fourth by a long strip of railway track.

Below: Spectators swarm across the 3rd green during the 1947 Match Play Championship.
Opposite page: Jack Nicklaus tees off during the '96 Open.

ROYAL ST GEORGE'S

Royal St George's - often simply called Sandwich after the neighbouring seaside town - was originally laid out by Laidlaw Purves in 1887 and has been changed little since. It was the first English venue for the Open, in 1894, and the Championship has returned there often since. In 1985, Sandy Lyle won here, the first British victory in the Open for 16 years. The great golfer Henry Cotton won his first Open title at Sandwich, and he described it as as being a 'golfer's heaven'.

Below: The 60-foot bunker at the 4th - reputedly the deepest in the UK.

ROYAL TROON

In 1978 Troon Golf Club celebrated its centenary year and as such was given its Royal title. It is at the southern end of a number of links courses which hug the western coast of Scotland and views from Troon include the ghostly Ailsa Craig and the arresting hills of the Isle of Arran. The layout of the course has evolved over time with input from some of the finest course architects: James Braid, Frank Pennink and Alister Mackenzie, the designer of both Augusta and Cypress Point in the States. As a result, Troon is a tough and challenging course.

Troon is home to both the longest and the shortest holes in Open Championship courses: the 6th hole is 577 yards long and known as Turnberry, the shortest, at only 126 yards is the 'Postage Stamp' and, although Gene Sarazen made his famous hole-in-one here in 1973, the hole is deceptively deadly.

SUNNINGDALE

Reputedly one of the best inland courses in Britain, Sunningdale was built in 1900. The Old Course was designed by Willie Park Jr, the first modern golf architect, while the New Course, added in 1922, was designed by Harry Colt. Sunningdale is not long enough to stretch today's 'power hitters', and it is no longer included in the Championship rota, but it remains a course of beauty and subtlety, and offers plenty of challenges to the average golfer.

Above: Aerial view of Royal Troon, which stretches along the beach on the Western coast of Scotland. Founded in 1878, it received its Royal title in its centenary year.

TURNBERRY

The Ailsa course at the Turnberry Hotel was built at the turn of the century and named after the Marquis of Ailsa, who commissioned it. With the coming of the hotel in 1907, Turnberry became one of the first hotel/golf resorts in the in the world. The Open was first played there in 1977, and was memorable for the duel played out between Jack Nicklaus and Tom Watson. Since then the Championship has returned twice more, in 1986 and 1994.

Top: The new clubhouse was opened in 1993, in time for the following year's Open.
Right: The Turnberry Lighthouse.

WENTWORTH

Wentworth, founded in the 1920s and now one of the best-known courses in Britain, is also the venue for the PGA Championship. The West Course - which is the one everybody has in mind when they speak of Wentworth - was designed by the famous golf architect Harry S. Colt in 1923, and it is still one of the longest and toughest in Britain.

Above: Costantino Rocca plays out of a bunker onto the 14th green during the 1995 Toyota World Match Play.

ST ANDREWS

G iven the expectations of most visitors to what is acknowledged to be the 'home of golf', St Andrews can, at first glance, seem a bleak and ordinary piece of land. It is the most revered of courses; all golfers serious about their game make the pilgrimage to the Old course. It was here that the Royal and Ancient Golf Club, first founded in 1754, convened to regularise the game and draw up the rules that form the basis of those used today. Golf has been played here since around 1400AD and the course remains open to the public, the St Andrews Links Trust having been created in 1874 by an Act of Parliament.

The granite grey clubhouse looms over the wide 'Valley of Sin', where both the 1st and the 18th holes are dissected by Swilcan Burn. Its many treacherous hazards

include the bunker 'Hell' which guards the 14th hole, the Cockle bunker at the 7th and the Strath bunker in front of the 11th. It is on the 17th where many of the world's champions have come unstuck, at the notorious Road Hole bunker, among them, Arnold Palmer and Tom Watson - strike too hard to miss the bunker and you find yourself on the road. When the wind whips across this promontory of land in the River Eden Estuary, the whole course is truly formidable.

Despite fears that modern technology and advanced equipment may slowly erode the challenge of the course, there is no doubt that the magic of St Andrews will remain. With its five 18 hole courses and one 9 hole course, St Andrews Links is Europe's largest golf complex, with 99 holes of golf.

AUGUSTA

The Augusta National Golf Club started life as Fruitlands Nursery and was bought by Bobby Jones in 1931 as the location of his visionary course. The site was already beautiful, with established woodland and shrubs, including an avenue of magnolia trees leading to the colonial house. Along with the British course architect, Alister Mackenzie, Jones set about reworking the land into his own private haven. The course was principally designed by Mackenzie, and Jones assisted by playing thousands of experimental shots to ensure that the course was as challenging as it was dramatic.

Now home of the US Masters, which is held every spring when the course is at its blooming best, Augusta is appreciated for its strategic brilliance. Temptations lurk for the unwary golfer and players are required to think through every shot carefully before addressing the ball. Jones claimed that it was possible to birdie at each hole, yet it was also just as possible to double-bogey every hole.

MEDINAH

It would seem an unlikely place to find a Moorish temple and a course built for the use of the Ancient Arabic Order of Nobles of the Mystic Shrine, but Medinah Number 3 is situated in the suburbs of Chicago. Built in the decadent 1920's as a private club for the 'Shriners,' it has been the host of three US Opens. The course itself is a challenging one, making full use of Lake Kadijah as a potential pitfall. Initially intended for use by women, the course was handed over to the men as it was deemed by the ladies to be too difficult!

MERION

Merion Golf Club in Pennsylvania has been witness to two of golf's great events. It was in the 1930 Amateur that Bobby Jones beat Eugene Holmes to claim his Grand Slam; he had played his first tournament here in 1916, aged just 14. The other legendary moment played out at Merion was in 1950, when Ben Hogan made his valiant comeback only a year after the car crash that almost killed him. It was the US Open and Hogan was victorious.

Initially a cricket club, the course, with its short holes, has begun to show its age – today's equipment makes such designs seem less challenging and it has not held an US Open since 1981. It is, however, a classic course, right down to the little wicker baskets, rather than flags, that sit atop the pins.

OAKMONT

Oakmont's designers Henry and William Fownes wanted their course to be punishing and they succeeded with this course in Pennsylvania. Known for its fast greens and its multitude of bunkers, the course is generally believed to be the most difficult 18 holes in the USA. When it was built it had over 300 bunkers, that number has since been reduced, but it still boasts the infamous 'church pews' bunker, seven parallel ridges of grass and sand.

Some of the greatest names in golf have triumphed at Oakmont: Bobby Jones, Ben Hogan, Jack Nicklaus, and Johnny Miller and in 1987 the course was designated a National Historic Landmark, the only golf course in the US to be so honoured.

PEBBLE BEACH

Along the spectacular rocky shore of Carmel Bay on the Monterey Peninsula, California, Pebble Beach Golf Links is as beautiful as it is demanding. Many an 'invincible' player has come unstuck here: Bobby Jones in the 1929 Amateur and Jack Nicklaus in the 1982 US Open are the most famous. It has also been a scene of triumph for many, including Tiger Woods' victories in the US Open and the AT and T Championships of 2000.

The course is buffeted by the Pacific Ocean and surrounded by pines and many of its holes lie against the coast line. The 17th hole in particular is renowned for its windy cliff top position, although Tom Watson overcame the challenge to birdie this hole and win the 1982 Open.

PINE VALLEY

As its name suggests, Pine Valley is an inland course surrounded by dense pine forest in the south of New Jersey. The brainchild of a wealthy Philadelphian, George Crump, who spotted the site from the window of a railway carriage; the course has been accused of being the biggest bunker in the world. Its island fairways and greens demand very precise play and its ability to terrify even the most confident players has earned it a reputation as a psychological challenge. Just taking a look at the nicknames for the bunkers and holes reinforces this opinion: one bunker on the tenth hole is known as the 'Devil's Arse' while the seventh hole is dominated by a desert of sand known as 'Hell's half acre.'

SHINNECOCK HILLS

Shinnecock Hills was America's first 18 hole course, forged from low-lying sand hills on Long Island in 1891. Its Scottish designer, Willie Dunn had been commissioned to build a course for William K Vanderbilt, heir to the famous business empire and on its completion it became a fashionable and exclusive club, where the wealthy members could enjoy a game whilst wearing their customary red coats.

Legend has it that Dunn had shaped many of the bunkers from Indian burial mounds scattered across the site and that it was not unusual for golfers to find human bones in the sand. Dunn's original course has undergone some updating to recompense for the development of the game and in 1984 the US Open returned to Shinnecock despite concerns that it could not accommodate a modern championship.

KIAWAH ISLAND

K iawah Island was built to house the 1991 Ryder Cup and has a reputation as America's toughest resort course. The 17th has claimed many famous casualties when the wind is blowing hard, since it has to be played over water and into the wind. As a modern course it looks very different from more traditional links in Britain - and in fact when it first opened one player commented that it "looked like something from Mars".

MAJOR
COMPETITIONS

₤ OPEN CHAMPIONSHIP

The gentleman golfers of Scotland enjoyed competing and at the suggestion of Major J. O. Fairlie, the secretary of Prestwick Golf Club, a tournament was organised to decide who was the best professional. In 1860, eight pros turned up to play at Prestwick. The winner, Willie Park, beat Old Tom Morris by two strokes and received as his prize an unusual red Moroccan leather belt ornamented with silver plaques illustrating golfing scenes. Although the tournament wasn't strictly 'open', the first of the British Open Championships had been won. In the following year the competition was opened up to anyone 'in the world' who wanted to play, probably as a result of the amateurs' desire to have a go at beating the professionals. The prize belt was presented again, this time to Old Tom, and it was decreed that the belt would be given permanently to any competitor who succeeded in winning three successive Opens – surely an impossible feat! When Old Tom's son, Young Tom was permanently awarded the belt in 1870 the organisers, consisting of the R&A, the Honourable Company of Edinburgh Golfers and Prestwick, took a year to raise the money for the new prize, a silver claret jug that is still used to this day.

THE PRICE OF VICTORY

Prize money was introduced to the tournament in 1863, although the winner could only expect to receive the belt. The following year the winner was awarded £6 from a total fund of £12. In 1892, this amount was increased to an enormous £100. This was the same year in which an entry fee was charged, as a result of the large number of contestants. In 2002, the total amount of prize money available was £3.85 million, with the winner, Ernie Els, receiving a cheque for £700,000. Many contestants now need to pass through qualifying rounds in order to compete. Such impressive amounts of money were not always on offer for the winner of the Open. The R&A, who took over the administration of the competition in 1919, recognised that investment was required if the Open was to continue as a serious tournament. It was the prestige of the tournament which ultimately kept it popular.

The first American to win the trophy was Jock Hutchison, an expatriate Scot. He won in 1921, and this began a period of domination by US players. The following year the claret jug was presented to the flamboyant Walter Hagen, who succeeded in winning the Open another three times. Despite Hagen's success, the Open was unpopular with American players who were often unwilling to cross the Atlantic to

play on unfamiliar links courses for what they considered to be meagre amounts. When Ben Hogan arrived in 1953 to take his turn at holding the trophy, he was a rare American contender. Despite this, very few Britons managed to win on home soil. Players such as Peter Thompson of Australia and Bobby Locke of South Africa dominated the competition during the fifties. The Open was never

Above: Greg Norman putts on the final green during the 1993 Open at Royal St George's, as the capacity crowd holds its breath. He went on to beat world champion Nick Faldo, with the lowest closing round by an Open winner in the 133-year history of the Championship to date.

at risk of dying, but in 1960, when Arnold Palmer crossed the Atlantic, his arrival heralded a new era for the tournament. Palmer brought not only a wealth of interest, he also persuaded his compatriots to travel too. His successive wins in 1961 and 1962 were played out in front of television cameras and as he was followed by players such as Nicklaus, Trevino and Watson, the British Open was revived.

The tournament has been dominated by professionals, only three amateurs have ever won: John Ball in 1890, Harold Hilton in 1892 and 1897 and the greatest ever Amateur, Bobby Jones in 1926, 1927 and 1930. Of the professionals who have held the title, only a small number have achieved outstanding success. Harry Vardon holds the record for number of victories, he won in 1896, 1898, 1899, 1903, 1911 and 1914. Tom Morris's four successive victories have never been equalled, and only four players have won the title five times in their careers: J. H. Taylor, James Braid, Peter Thompson and Tom Watson. The youngest ever champion was Young Tom Morris, who was only 17 years old when he won in 1868 and the oldest champion was his father, Old Tom Morris, who won the belt in 1867 aged 46.

THE OPEN CHAMPIONSHIP

RESULTS

Year	Venue	Winner	Score	Year	Venue	Winner	Score
1860	Prestwick	Willie Park Snr	174	1898	Prestwick	Harry Vardon	307
1861	Prestwick	Tom Morris Snr	163	1899	St George's (Sandwich)	Harry Vardon	310
1862	Prestwick	Tom Morris Snr	163	1900	St Andrews	JH Taylor	309
1863	Prestwick	Willie Park Snr	168	1901	Muirfield	James Braid	309
1864	Prestwick	Tom Morris Snr	167	1902	R Liverpool (Holylake)	Sandy Herd	307
1865	Prestwick	Andrew Strath	162	1903	Prestwick	Harry Vardon	300
1866	Prestwick	Willie Park Snr	169	1904	R George's (Sandwich)	Jack White	296
1867	Prestwick	Tom Morris Snr	170	1905	St Andrews	James Braid	318
1868	Prestwick	Tom Morris Jnr	157	1906	Muirfield	James Braid	300
1869	Prestwick	Tom Morris Jnr	154	1907	R Liverpool (Holylake)	Arnaud Massy (Fr)	312
1870	Prestwick	Tom Morris Jnr	149	1908	Prestwick	James Braid	291
1871	No competition			1909	Cinque Ports (Deal)	JH Taylor	295
1872	Prestwick	Tom Morris Jnr	166	1910	St Andrews	James Braid	299
1873	St Andrews	Tom Kidd	179	1911	R George's (Sandwich)	Harry Vardon	303
1874	Musselburgh	Mungo Park	159	1912	Muirfield	Ted Ray	295
1875	Prestwick	Willie Park Snr	166	1913	R Liverpool (Holylake)	JH Taylor	304
1876	St Andrews	Bob Martin	176	1914	Prestwick	Harry Vardon	306
1877	R Musselburgh	Jamie Anderson	160	1920	Cinque Ports (Deal)	George Duncan	303
1878	Prestwick	Jamie Anderson	157	1921	St Andrews	Jock Hutchison (US)	296*
1879	St Andrews	Jamie Anderson	169	1922	R George's (Sandwich)	Walter Hagen (US)	300
1880	R Musselburgh	Bob Ferguson	162	1923	Troon	Arthur Havers	295
1881	Prestwick	Bob Ferguson	170	1924	R Liverpool (Holylake)	Walter Hagen (US)	301
1882	St Andrews	Bob Ferguson	171	1925	Prestwick	Jim Barnes *** (US)	300
1883	R Musselburgh	Willie Fernie	159*	1926	R Lytham & St Annes	Bobby Jones *** (US)	291
1884	Prestwick	Jack Simpson	160	1927	St Andrews	Bobby Jones *** (US)	285
1885	St Andrews	Bob Martin	171	1928	R George's (Sandwich)	Walter Hagen (US)	292
1886	R Musselburgh	David Brown	157	1929	Muirfield	Walter Hagen (US)	292
1887	Prestwick	Willie Park Jnr	161	1930	R Liverpool (Holylake)	Bobby Jones (US)	291
1888	St Andrews	Jack Burns	171	1931	Carnoustie	Tommy Armour (US)	296
1889	R Musselburgh	Willie Park Jnr	155*	1932	Prince's (Sandwich)	Gene Sarazen (US)	283
1890	Prestwick	John Ball	164	1933	St Andrews	Densmore Shute (US)	292*
1891	St Andrews	Hugh Kirkaldy	166	1934	R George's (Sandwich)	Henry Cotton	283
1892	Muirfield	Harold Hilton	305**	1935	Muirfield	Alf Perry	283
1893	Prestwick	W Auchterlonie	322	1936	R Liverpool (Holylake)	Alf Padgham	287
1894	St George's (Sandwich)	JH Taylor	326	1937	Carnoustie	Henry Cotton	290
1895	St Andrews	JH Taylor	322	1938	R St George's	Reg Whitcombe	295
1896	Muirfield	Harry Vardon	316*	1939	St Andrews	Dick Burton	290
1897	R Liverpool (Holylake)	Harold Hilton	~314	1946	St Andrews	Sam Snead (US)	290

YEAR	VENUE	WINNER	SCORE	YEAR	VENUE	WINNER	SCORE
1947	R Liverpool (Holylake)	Fred Daly	293	1990	St Andrews	Nick Faldo	270
1948	Muirfield	Henry Cotton	284	1991	Royal Birkdale	Ian Baker-Finch (Aus)	272
1949	R George's (Sandwich)	Bobby Locke (SA)	3*	1992	Muirfield	Nick Faldo	272
1950	Troon	Bobby Locke (SA)	279	1993	R George's (Sandwich)	Greg Norman (Aus)	267
1951	Royal Portrush	Max Faulkner	285	1994	Turnberry	Nick Price (Zim)	268
1952	R Lytham & St Annes	Bobby Locke (SA)	287	1995	St Andrews	John Daly (US)	282*
1953	Carnoustie	Ben Hogan (US)	282	1996	R Lytham & St Annes	Tom Lehman (US)	271
1954	Royal Birkdale	Peter Thomson (Aus)	283	1997	Royal Troon	Justin Leonard (US)	272
1955	St Andrews	Peter Thomson (Aus)	281	1998	Royal Birkdale	Mark O'Meara (US)	280*
1956	R Liverpool (Holylake)	Peter Thomson (Aus)	286	1999	Carnoustie	Paul Lawrie	290*
1957	St Andrews	Bobby Locke (SA)	297	2000	St Andrews	Tiger Woods (US)	269
1958	R Lytham & St Annes	Peter Thomson (Aus)	278*	2001	R Lytham & St Annes	David Duval	274
1959	Muirfield	Gary Player (SA)	284	2002	Muirfield	Ernie Els	278
1960	St Andrews	Kel Nagle (Aus)	278				
1961	Royal Birkdale	Arnold Palmer (US)	284	R Royal		***amateur	*play-off
1962	Troon	Arnold Palmer (US)	276				
1963	R Lytham & St Annes	Bob Charles (NZ)	277*				
1964	St Andrews	Tony Lema (US)	279				
1965	Royal Birkdale	Peter Thomson (Aus)	285				
1966	Muirfield	Jack Nicklaus (US)	282				
1967	R Liverpool (Holylake)	Roberto de Vicenzo (Arg)	278				
1968	Carnoustie	Gary Player (SA)	289				
1969	R Lytham & St Annes	Tony Jacklin	280				
1970	St Andrews	Jack Nicklaus (US)	283*				
1971	Royal Birkdale	Lee Trevino (US)	278				
1972	Muirfield	Lee Trevino (US)	278				
1973	Troon	Tom Weiskopf (US)	276				
1974	R Lytham & St Annes	Gary Player (SA)	282				
1975	Carnoustie	Tom Watson (US)	279*				
1976	Royal Birkdale	Johnny Miller (US)	279				
1977	Turnberry	Tom Watson (US)	268				
1978	St Andrews	Jack Nicklaus (US)	281				
1979	R Lytham & St Annes	Seve Ballesteros (Sp)	283				
1980	Muirfield	Tom Watson (US)	271				
1981	R George's (Sandwich)	Bill Rogers (US)	276				
1982	Royal Troon	Tom Watson (US)	284				
1983	Royal Birkdale	Tom Watson (US)	275				
1984	St Andrews	Seve Ballesteros (Sp)	276				
1985	R George's (Sandwich)	Sandy Lyle	282				
1986	Turnberry	Greg Norman (Aus)	280				
1987	Muirfield	Nick Faldo	279				
1988	R Lytham & St Annes	Seve Ballesteros (Sp)	273				
1989	Royal Troon	Mark Calcavecchia (US)	275*				

OPEN RECORDS

Most wins: 6, Harry Vardon (GB)
                      1896, 1898, 1899, 1903, 1911,
                      1914

Biggest victory margin: 13 strokes, Tom Morris Snr (GB)
                      1862

THE US OPEN CHAMPIONSHIP

The first US Open Championship took place at Newport, Rhode Island in 1895, the day after the first US Amateur Championship was held on the same course. The winner was Harry Rawlins, an English born professional who worked at the club. For the following 15 years, the event was dominated by expatriate Britons, many of them Scottish. The most renowned of these was Harry Vardon, who entered the tournament in 1900 as a break from a series of exhibitions and proceeded to win it. His victory helped to make the US Open as valued an event as its British cousin. In 1911, the Championship was finally won by a native, Johnny McDermott at Chicago, and then at Brookline in 1913, Francis Ouimet routed the cream of the British crop, Harry Vardon and Ted Ray, to win a dramatic victory.

Like the British Open, the US Open is a strokeplay tournament, where an individual plays four rounds of 18 holes in as few shots as possible. Initially the Championship was played over 36 holes rather than 72, with a 36 hole play off in the event of a tie. By 1931, four rounds was the regulation. However the 36 hole play-off had to be abandoned following a game that lasted for 144 holes: the initial 72 holes plus two play-offs of 36 holes each. Such a marathon was considered unrepeatable and with that there was a return to 18 hole play-offs.

That same year, American clubs began to open up their clubhouses, finally emancipating the professional golfers. As in Britain, the US Open was dominated by professional players, with only eight victories going to amateurs. Again, Bobby Jones was the most successful of these, accumulating four wins in his brief career. In one well known incident during the second round of the 1925 Championship, Jones called a shot penalty on himself when his ball moved slightly as he addressed it. Golf is a game that engenders scrupulous honesty; no-one had seen Jones's ball move, yet he would not cheat. He lost the trophy to Willie MacFarlane.

Four wins is the highest number of victories yet achieved in the US Open and only four players have achieved this feat. Along with Bobby Jones is Willie Anderson who won in 1901 and then from 1903 to 1905, the only player to have managed three successive wins. Ben Hogan and Jack Nicklaus keep Anderson and Jones company. In 2000 the player who won the open by a record 15 strokes was Tiger Woods, the man most likely to succeed at beating the record first set by Anderson. At his current age of 28, he has already won two US Opens.

Above: Gary Player won the US open in 1965 at Bellerive. Player is one of only five men to win all four majors - the others are Jack Nicklaus, Gene Sarazen, Ben Hogan, and Tiger Woods.

THE US OPEN CHAMPIONSHIP RESULTS

WINNERS US, EXCEPT WHERE STATED

Year	Venue	Winner	Score	Year	Venue	Winner	Score
1895	Newport	Horace Rawlins	173	1935	Oakmont	Sam Parks	299
1896	Shinnecock Hills	James Foulis	152	1936	Baltusrol	Tony Manero	282
1897	Chicago	Joe Lloyd	162	1937	Oakland Hills	Ralph Guldahl	281
1898	Myopia Hunt	Fred Herd	328**	1938	Cherry Hills	Ralph Guldahl	284
1899	Baltimore	Willie Smith	315	1939	Philadelphia	Byron Nelson	284*
1900	Chicago	Harry Vardon (GB)	313	1940	Canterbury	Lawson Little	287*
1901	Myopia Hunt	Willie Anderson	331*	1941	Colonial	Craig Wood	284
1902	Garden City	Laurie Auchterlonie	307	1946	Canterbury	Lloyd Mangrum	284*
1903	Baltusrol	Willie Anderson	307*	1947	St Louis	Lew Worsham	282*
1904	Glen View	Willie Anderson	303	1948	Riviera	Ben Hogan	276
1905	Myopia Hunt	Willie Anderson	314	1949	Medinah	Cary Middlecoff	286
1906	Onwentsia	Alex Smith	295	1950	Merion	Ben Hogan	287*
1907	Philadelphia	Alex Ross	302	1951	Oakland Hills	Ben Hogan	287
1908	Myopia Hunt	Fred McLeod	322*	1952	Northwood	Julius Boros	281
1909	Englewood	George Sargent	290	1953	Oakmont	Ben Hogan	283
1910	Philadelphia	Alex Smith	298*	1954	Baltusrol	Ed Furgol	284
1911	Chicago	John McDermott	307*	1955	Olympic	Jack Fleck	287*
1912	Buffalo	John McDermott	294	1956	Oak Hill	Cary Middlecoff	281
1913	Brookline	Francis Quimet ***	304*	1957	Inverness	Dick Mayer	282*
1914	Midlothian	Walter Hagen	290	1958	Southern Hills	Tommy Bolt	283
1915	Baltusrol	Jerome Travers ***	297	1959	Winged Foot	Billy Casper	282
1916	Minikahda	Chick Evans ***	286	1960	Cherry Hills	Arnold Palmer	280
1919	Brae Burn	Walter Hagen	301*	1961	Oakland Hills	Gene Littler	281
1920	Inverness	Ted Ray (GB)	295	1962	Oakmont	Jack Nicklaus	283*
1921	Columbia	Jim Barnes	289	1963	Brookline	Julius Boros	293*
1922	Skokie	Gene Sarazen	288	1964	Congressional	Ken Venturi	278
1923	Inwood	Bobby Jones ***	296*	1965	Bellerive	Gary Player (SA)	282*
1924	Oakland Hills	Cyril Walker	297	1966	Olympic	Billy Casper	278*
1925	Worcester	Willie McFarlane	291*	1967	Baltusrol	Jack Nicklaus	275
1926	Scioto	Bobby Jones	~293	1968	Oak Hill	Lee Trevino	275
1927	Oakmont	Tommy Armour	301*	1969	Champions	Orville Moody	281
1928	Olympia Fields	Johnny Farrell	294*	1970	Hazeltine	Tony Jacklin (GB)	281
1929	Winged Foot	Bobby Jones ***	294*	1971	Merion	Lee Trevino	280*
1930	Interlachen	Bobby Jones ***	287	1972	Pebble Beach	Jack Nicklaus	290
1931	Inverness	Billy Burke	292*	1973	Oakmont	Johnny Miller	279
1932	Fresh Meadow	Gene Sarazen	286	1974	Winged Foot	Hale Irwin	287
1933	North Shore	Johnny Goodman ***	287	1975	Medinah	Lou Graham	287*
1934	Merion	Olin Dutra	293	1976	Atlanta	Jerry Pate	277

Year	Venue	Winner	Score
1977	Southern Hills	Hubert Green	278
1978	Cherry Hills	Andy North	285
1979	Inverness	Hale Irwin	284
1980	Baltusrol	Jack Nicklaus	272
1981	Merion	David Graham (Aus)	273
1982	Pebble Beach	Tom Watson	282
1983	Oakmont	Larry Nelson	280
1984	Winged Foot	Fuzzy Zoeller	276*
1985	Oakland Hills	Andy North	279
1986	Shinnecock Hills	Ray Floyd	279
1987	Olympic	Scott Simpson	277
1988	Brookline	Curtis Strange	278*
1989	Oak Hill	Curtis Strange	278
1990	Medinah	Hale Irwin	280*
1991	Hazeltine, Minn.	Payne Stewart	282
1992	Pebble Beach	Tom Kite	285
1993	Baltusrol	Lee Janzen	272
1994	Oakmont	Ernie Els (SA)	279
1995	Shinnecock Hills	Corey Pavin	280
1996	Oakland Hills	Steve Jones	278
1997	Congressional	Ernie Els (SA)	276
1998	Olympic	Lee Janzen	280
1999	Pinehurst	Payne Stewart	279
2000	Pebble Beach	Tiger Woods	272
2001	Southern Hills	Retief Goosen	276
2002	Farmingdale	Tiger Woods	277

1917-1918 not played (First World War)
1942-1945 not played (Second World War)
*play-off
**competition extended over 77 holes
***amateur

US OPEN RECORDS

Most wins: 4

Willie Anderson (US)
1901, 1903, 1904, 1905

Bobby Jones (US)
1923, 1926, 1929, 1930

Ben Hogan (US)
1948, 1950, 1951, 1953

Jack Nicklaus (US)
1962, 1967, 1972, 1980

Biggest victory margin: 15 shots
Tiger Woods (US) 2000

Right: Gene Sarazen just
after winning the US
Open Trophy in 1932

THE MASTERS TOURNAMENT

T he Masters is a tournament that is unique in many ways. The youngest of the four Majors, it was inaugurated in 1934, the brainchild of Bobby Jones. Following his retirement in 1930, Jones had his own private course built at his hometown in Georgia. Jones had been one of the greatest players of his age and as a result hugely popular, however he hated receiving attention from the public. His course was to be a haven for himself and his friends and this exclusive air remains at Augusta National. The tournament that Jones hosted was a private affair, a gathering of 72 players who were present by invitation only. The press labelled the tournament 'The Masters' because those 72 players included the best golfers in the world. Jones apparently disliked the label, considering it pretentious, but it has stuck and now the US Masters is played at Augusta every year, in April.

The tournament retains its old fashioned and traditional flavour. No advertising is permitted at Augusta; admission as a spectator is difficult to acquire and regulated with a limited-badge system. There are no pre-qualifying events and entry into the Masters tournament is difficult, to say the least. The invitations are now issued by a committee and the criteria for automatic admission are stringent: the top 24 finishers at the previous Masters automatically enter, but only if they are American. Foreign players are admitted by invitation only.

MASTER OF AUGUSTA

The Masters has not been without controversy. Augusta National is situated in the Deep South. In the early 1970s, civil rights campaigners and Congress alleged that the Masters was a discriminatory institution; no black golfer had ever been admitted. In 1971, Jones's partner, and the 'master' of Augusta Clifford Roberts, expanded the qualification categories, any winner of a US Tour event could enter and, in 1975, Lee Elder, having won the Monsanto Open, became the first black player. Tiger Woods's first victory came in 1997 and he has dominated the tournament in the twenty-first century, dismissing all accusations of prejudice. Roberts and Jones had very publicly fallen out in 1968 and never spoke to each other again. Jones died in 1971, and Roberts continued to rule over Augusta with an iron fist. His reign ended in 1977 when he walked out onto the course one evening and shot himself.

Once a player wins at Augusta, he is honoured by being presented with a green club jacket at an award ceremony that echoes the coronation of royalty! Traditionally, the winner keeps the jacket for one year before returning it to the Augusta. Jack Nicklaus has won at the Masters six times, as yet an unequalled record and like all other winners has received the silver replica of the clubhouse that acts as trophy. The tournament has been dominated by American players and Gary Player was the first non-American to win it in 1961. Since then, foreign players have begun to have an impact on the tournament; Europeans such as Ballesteros, Olazabal and Langer have enjoyed success and in 1989, Nick Faldo became the first British winner, he went on to win the tournament twice more. With Vijay Singh becoming the first man from Australasia to win in 2000, the event has clearly acquired global respectability.

THE MASTERS RESULTS

Year	Winner	Score	Year	Winner	Score	Year	Winner	Score
1934	Horton Smith	284	1961	Gary Player (SA)	280	1985	Bernard Langer (Ger)	282
1935	Gene Sarazen	282*	1962	Arnold Palmer	280*	1986	Jack Nicklaus	279
1936	Horton Smith	285	1963	Jack Nicklaus	286	1987	Larry Mize	285*
1937	Byron Nelson	283	1964	Arnold Palmer	276	1988	Sandy Lyle (GB)	281
1938	Henry Picard	285	1965	Jack Nicklaus	271	1989	Nick Faldo (GB)	283*
1939	Ralph Guldahl	279	1966	Jack Nicklaus	288*	1990	Nick Faldo (GB)	278*
1940	Jimmy Demaret	280	1967	Gay Brewer	280	1991	Ian Woosnam (GB)	277
1941	Craig Wood	280	1968	Bob Goalby	277	1992	Fred Couples	275
1942	Byron Nelson	280*	1969	George Archer	281	1993	Bernhard Langer (Ger)	277
1946	Herman Keiser	282	1970	Billy Casper	279*	1994	Jose-Maria Olazabal (Sp)	279
1947	Jimmy Demaret	281	1971	Charles Coody	279	1995	Ben Crenshaw	274
1948	Claude Harmon	279	1972	Jack Nicklaus	286	1996	Nick Faldo (GB)	276
1949	Sam Snead	282	1973	Tommy Aaron	283	1997	Tiger Woods	270
1950	Jimmy Demaret	281	1974	Gary Player (SA)	278	1998	Mark O'Meara	279
1951	Ben Hogan	274	1975	Jack Nicklaus	276	1999	Jose-Maria Olazabal (Sp)	280
1952	Sam Snead	286	1976	Ray Floyd	271	2000	Vijay Singh (Fij)	278
1953	Ben Hogan	274	1977	Tom Watson	276	2001	Tiger Woods	272
1954	Sam Snead	289*	1978	Gary Player (SA)	277	2002	Tiger Woods	276
1955	Cary Middlecoff	279	1979	Fuzzy Zoeller	280*	2003	Mike Weir	
1956	Jack Burke	289	1980	Seve Ballesteros (Sp)	280			*play-off
1957	Doug Ford	283	1981	Tom Watson	280		Most wins: 6, Jack Nicklaus (US)	
1958	Arnold Palmer	284	1982	Craig Stadler	284*		1963, 1965, 1966, 1972, 1975, 1986	
1959	Art Wall	284	1983	Seve Ballesteros (Sp)	280		Biggest victory margin: 12 shots,	
1960	Arnold Palmer	282	1984	Ben Crenshaw	277		Tiger Woods (Above) (US) 1997	

THE US PGA CHAMPIONSHIP

I n 1916, the Professional Golfers' Association of America was formed and they celebrated their inauguration with the first Professional Golfers Championship. The US PGA began life as a matchplay event, which made it exciting and highly unpredictable. However, in 1953, six former champions were knocked out in the first two rounds and with the added incentive of television viewers requiring a game that would remain exciting until the end and which included the stars, the format was changed. In 1958 the tournament became strokeplay over 72 holes.

The tournament is important to professionals because the winner automatically qualifies for all PGA tournaments for life, thus avoiding the anxiety of pre-qualification rounds. However, the tournament is usually considered the least important of the four Majors; an August event, in the calendar it sits far too close to the Open held in July and has in the past clashed with the British event, most notably in 1953 when Ben Hogan chose to travel to Carnoustie rather than remain in the States for the PGA.

Qualification to the PGA is determined by players' performance on the US PGA Tour, which results in it being a mostly American event. Some of the greatest names in the game have competed for the title: Walter Hagen won the Championship five times, a record that was equalled by Jack Nicklaus. Gene Sarazen and Sam Snead each won three PGAs. The calibre of applicants is clearly high, however the tournament also has a reputation of introducing relative unknowns to the limelight. Many PGA winners are collecting a Major for the first and, perhaps, the only time, David Toms, Rich Beem and Davis Love III are good recent examples.

This combination of legendary and ordinary winners adds kudos to the tournament and gives up and coming stars a huge incentive. Tiger Woods has already won two PGAs with undoubtedly more to follow. The only notable name that is missing is that of Bobby Jones, as an amateur he was forbidden to enter.

RESULTS

Year	Venue	Winner	Margin/Score	Year	Venue	Winner	Margin/Score
1916	Siwanoy	Jim Barnes	1 up	1921	Inwood	Walter Hagen	3 & 2
1919	Engineers	Jim Barnes	6 & 5	1922	Oakmont	Gene Sarazen	4 & 3
1920	Flossmoor	Jock Hitchinson	1 up	1923	Pelham	Gene Sarazen	4 &3
				1924	French	LickWalter Hagen	2 up

Year	Venue	Winner	Score
1925	Olympia Fields	Walter Hagen	6 & 5
1926	Salisbury	Walter Hagen	5 & 3
1927	Cedar Crest	Walter Hagen	1 up
1928	Five Farms	Leo Diegel	6 & 5
1929	Hillcrest	Leo Diegel	6 & 4
1930	Fresh Meadow	Tommy Armour	1 up
1931	Wannamoisett	Tom Creavy	2 & 1
1932	Keller	Olin Durra	4 & 3
1933	Blue Mound	Gene Sarazen	5 & 4
1934	Park	Paul Runyan at	38th
1935	Twin Hills	Johnny Revolta	5 & 4
1936	Pinehurst	Densmore Shute	3 & 2
1937	Pittsburgh	Densmore Shute at	37th
1938	Shawnee	Paul Runyan	8 & 7
1939	Pomonok	Henry Picard at	37th
1940	Hershey	Byron Nelson	1 up
1941	Cherry Hills	Vic Ghezzi at	38th
1942	Seaview	Sam Snead	2 & 1
1944	Manito	Bob Hamilton	1 up
1945	Morraine	Bryon Nelson	4 & 3
1946	Portland	Ben Hogan	6 & 4
1947	Plum Hollow	Jim Ferrier	2 & 1
1948	Norwood Hills	Ben Hogan	7 & 6
1949	Hermitage	Sam Snead	3 & 2
1950	Scioto	Chandler Harper	4 & 3
1951	Oakmont	Sam Snead	7 & 6
1952	Big Spring	Jim Turnesa	1 up
1953	Birmingham	Walter Burkemo	2 & 1
1954	Keller	Chick Harbert	4 & 3
1955	Meadowbrook	Doug Ford	4 & 3
1956	Blue Hill	Jack Burke	3 & 2
1957	Miami Valley	Lionel Hebert	2 & 1
1958	Llanerch Dow	Finsterwald	276
1959	Minneapolis	Bob Rosburg	277
1960	Firestone	Jay Herbert	281
1961	Olympia	Fields Jerry Barber	277*
1962	Aronimink	Gary Player (SA)	278
1963	Dallas	Jack Nicklaus	279
1964	Columbus	Bobby Nichols	271
1965	Laurel Valley	Dave Marr	280
1966	Firestone	Al Geiberger	280
1967	Columbine	Don January	281*
1968	Pecan Valley	Julius Boros	281
1969	NCR (Dayton)	Ray Floyd	276
1970	Southern Hills	Dave Stockton	279
1971	PGA National**	Jack Nicklaus	281
1972	Oakland Hills	Gary Player (SA)	281
1973	Canterbury	Jack Nicklaus	277
1974	Tanglewood	Lee Trevino	276
1975	Firestone	Jack Nicklaus	277
1976	Congressional	Dave Stockton	281
1977	Pebble Beach	Lanny Wadkins	282*
1978	Oakmont	John Mahaffey	276*
1979	Oakland Hills	David Graham (Aus)	272*
1980	Oak Hill	Jack Nicklaus	274
1981	Atlanta	Larry Nelson	273
1982	Southern Hills	Ray Floyd	272
1983	Riviera	Hal Sutton	274
1984	Shoal Creek	Lee Trevino	273
1985	Cherry Hills	Hubert Green	278
1986	Inverness	Bob Tway	276
1987	PGA National**	Larry Nelson	287*
1988	Oak Tree	Jeff Sluman	272
1989	Kemper Lakes	Payne Stewart	276
1990	Shoal Creek	Wayne Grady (Aus)	282
1991	Crooked Stick	John Daly	276
1992	Bellerive	Nick Price (Zim)	278
1993	Inverness	Paul Azinger	272
1994	Southern Hills	Nick Price (Zim)	269
1995	Riviera	Steve Elkington (Aus)	267*
1996	Valhalla	Mark Brooks	277*
1997	Winged Foot	Davis Love III	269
1998	Sahalee	Vijay Singh (Fij)	271
1999	Medinah	Tiger Woods	277
2000	Valhalla	Tiger Woods	270
2001	Atlanta	David Toms	265
2002	Hazeltine	Rich Beem	278

*play-off   **PGA National (Palm Beach)

US PGA RECORDS

Most wins: 5,
Walter Hagen (US) 1921, 1924, 1925, 1926, 1927
Jack Nicklaus (US) 1963, 1971, 1973, 1975, 1980
Biggest victory margin:
matchplay, 8 & 7 Paul Runyan (US) 1938
strokeplay, 7 strokes Jack Nicklaus (US) 1980

THE RYDER CUP

I n 1926, Samuel Ryder, a prosperous seed merchant and Mayor of St. Albans was witness to an unofficial match at Wentworth between the British and US Professional Golf Associations. Ryder, a keen golfer himself, was so impressed by the contest, which was won by the British, 13 points to 1, that he was prompted to declare 'we must do this more often', and decided to donate the now famous gold cup as a trophy. Ryder may well have been influenced by the impressive British victory, but there can also be no denying that the team event sparked not only intense rivalry, but also fierce patriotism and camaraderie, hallmarks of the competition that remain to this day.

The first Ryder Cup match was held in 1927 at Worcester, Massachusetts and has since been a biennial event. Following their impressive victory the previous year, the British team fully expected to return with the cup, but were to be disappointed; the US won 9 to 2. However, in the 1929 return at Moortown, the British took their revenge and the cup was presented to the captain, George Duncan. Samuel Ryder never saw his home-side lose; he did not cross the Atlantic and did not live to see the first American win on British soil, at Southport and Ainsdale in 1937. In the decades before the war the competition was not only fierce but roughly equal. However, as with the Major tournaments, it soon became the clear that the Americans were dominating the Cup.

Below: Lord Wardington presents the Ryder trophy to Walter Hagen in 1937.
Opposite Page: Seve Ballesteros and Maria Olazabal in 1993.

AMERICAN DOMINATION

Between 1935 and 1977, the British managed only one victory, at Lindrick in 1957. There is good reason for this. World War II had taken its toll and post-war America was far stronger economically than ration-wracked Britain. While the United States was enjoying a golfing boom, British clubs were suffering from a lack of facilities and investment; it is little wonder that Ben Hogan complained about the their state. Great Britain and Ireland had come close to success in 1953, but lost out narrowly, by only one point. In 1957, the British team, under the inspired captainship of Dai Rees achieved a memorable win of 7"$^{1}/_{2}$ to 4$^{1}/_{2}$ in front of a cheering Yorkshire crowd at Lindrick. It would be 28 years before the USA was to concede defeat again. The lack of any real competition began to eat away at the popularity of the event. Matchplay competitions should be exciting, yet the Ryder was becoming yawningly predictable and repetitive. The first of two major changes to the competition was implemented in 1961, when all matches were reduced from 36 holes to 18, to increase the number of games and therefore the number of points available to fight for. Rather than giving the British an opportunity to win more games, it simply gave the Americans even more points. In 1963, at Atlanta, Arnold Palmer's team beat Great Britain & Ireland 23 points to 9.

Below: Bernard Langer misses a putt on the final hole of the Ryder Cup.

In 1969, the USA and Britain finally drew, but not without just a little controversy. It had all come down to the last match and, at the 18th hole, the teams were level as Jack Nicklaus and Tony Jacklin teed up. Imagine the tension as each man found himself on the green, level, with Nicklaus four feet from the hole and Jacklin just inches closer. Nicklaus holed his and then turned to his rival saying, "I don't think you'd have missed that Tony, but I'm not going to give you the chance"; a gesture of sportsmanship that has never been forgotten. The match was tied and the Cup shared, but Sam Snead, the US Captain, would never forgive Nicklaus for denying him a win on British soil.

Despite this, the Ryder Cup had become too dull to attract large audiences.

The British remained typically determined, continuing to throw themselves into the competition with eager hope; however,

Above: Gene Sarazen driving the first ball of the 1933 Ryder Cup in Southport. Great Britain won the match 6½-5½

American spectators were losing interest. And so, in 1979, the second major change was made to the competition: reinforcements were brought in.

FROM BRITAIN TO EUROPE

Ironically, it was an American who suggested that the Great Britain & Ireland be expanded to include golfers from the rest of Europe. In 1977, following another British defeat at Royal Lytham & St Annes, Jack Nicklaus approached Lord Derby, president of the PGA of Great Britain and argued the case for widening the selection process. There were good reasons for transforming the team into a European one: during the late seventies and eighties there was a wealth of European talent on offer; taking the Cup out to the continent would result in greater audience numbers and ultimately, America would face a more challenging opposition.

Once the trustees of Sam Ryder's relatives had approved the change, the first European team took to the course. Europe was still dominated by British players, but it also included a 22-year-old Seve Ballesteros. It was another win for the USA, but not quite as convincing as before. Another member of that Ryder Cup team was Tony Jacklin, playing in his seventh match. Jacklin was appointed captain for the first time in 1983 and not only was he experienced, he was hungry for victory. He gathered a team of the finest golfers on the continent, including Ballesteros, Faldo, Gallacher, Lyle, Langer, Torrance and Woosnam. Although the match was played at PGA National in Florida, it was a close call, the final result was USA 14^1/2 Europe 13^1/2. Suddenly, the Americans were not quite so comfortable.

The match in 1985 was held at the Belfry, the British home of the Ryder Cup. The European team consisted of almost the same golfers as the 1983 line-up, however, many of them had been collecting titles on American soil and now they were not just contenders, they were confident. The Americans were routed; the final putt was left to Sam Torrance and when he birdied to win his singles match, his tears of joy echoed the jubilation felt by everyone, Europe had come in from the cold.

It seems now that every Ryder Cup match is a grudge match. Golf is not normally a game that inspires patriotic fervour, aggressive tactics, green invasions. With it becoming more evenly competitive, the Ryder Cup has become a war, albeit a respectful and sporting one. That victory in 1985 was followed by an even more impressive one at Muirfield Village in 1989, when

Below: The '97 British Ryder Cup team.

Europe beat the USA on their own soil. In 1999, at the 'Battle of Brookline' the Americans staged an incredible comeback when the Americans had ended the second day of play down

Above: The 1935 British Ryder Cup Team included three Whitcombe brothers.

four points. Justin Leonard's winning putt prompted a green invasion that ruffled many feathers. The return match was postponed as a result of the September 11th attacks in New York, but in 2002, the Cup was to move home again.

THE CAPTAINS

Despite not hitting a shot themselves, the role of Ryder Cup captain is crucial. Chief motivators and man managers, it is their responsibility to get the best from each individual on the team. Captains submit the order of play for their team to the official and the matched lists result in the pairings. However, the pairings can be changed at anytime during the competition prior to a match beginning. The pairings for the fourballs and foursomes involve finding personalities that will complement one another; experienced players coax on rookies, aggressive shotmakers with metronomes who shoot every green in regulation, players on a winning streak partner less confident colleagues.

In 2002 at the Belfry, Sam Torrance, captaining for the first and, he says, the only time, gave a masterclass in the Captain's art. On paper the gulf between Britain

Olazabal, Clarke, were seemingly past their best or hopelessly out of form. The policy of selecting those who had enjoyed success on the European Tour resulted in the inclusion of players such as Pontypridd's Phillip Price, Dublin's Paul McGinley and Sweden's Niclas Fasth, while more illustrious golfers watched on television. By the end of the second day the teams were level. Since previous European successes had relied on getting a lead in the paired events and then clinging on to that advantage in the singles matches, the Europeans seemed in trouble. However, Torrance had a plan. Defying convention, he sent out his best players in the first few games hoping the momentum of early success would inspire those playing later. Lead by Colin Montgomerie's demolition of Scott Hoch, the points started to accumulate and the Americans wilted. Eventually the cup was secured by Price, turning over Phil Mickleson.

Without Torrance's inspired leadership, Europe may not have overturned the USA in 2002. For all Ryder Cup captains, the honour of leading their compatriots is second to none. Indeed, in golf, representative honours in the Ryder Cup are treasured.

Opposite Page: The 1985 British team went on Concorde; the 1959 team sailed the Queen Elizabeth. Below: Europe wins the Ryder in 1995.

THE RYDER CUP

RESULTS

Year	Venue	Winning Captain	Margin
1927	Worcester (Mass)	Walter Hagen(US)	$9^1/_2$-$2^1/_2$
1929	Moortown	George Duncan(GB)	7-5
1931	Scioto	Walter Hagen(US)	9-3
1933	Southport & Ainsdale	JH Taylor (GB)	*$6^1/_2$-$5^1/_2$
1935	Ridgewood	Walter Hagen(US)	9-3
1937	Southport & Ainsdale	Walter Hagen(US)	*8-4
1947	Portland	Ben Hogan(US)	11-1
1949	Ganton	Ben Hogan(US)	*7-5
1951	Pinehurst	Sam Snead(US)	$9^1/_2$-$2^1/_2$
1953	Wentworth	L Mangrum(US)	$6^1/_2$-$5^1/_2$
1955	Thunderbird**	Chick Harbert(US)	8-4
1957	Lindrick	Dai Rees(GB)	$7^1/_2$-$4^1/_2$
1959	Eldorado[1]	Sam Snead(US)	$8^1/_2$-$3^1/_2$
1961	RL&A[3]	Jerry Barber(US)	$14^1/_2$-$9^1/_2$
1963	East Lake(Atlanta)	Arnold Palmer(US)	23-9
1965	Royal Birkdale	B Nelson(US)	*$19^1/_2$-$12^1/_2$
1967	Champions[3]	Ben Hogan(US)	*$23^1/_2$-$8^1/_2$
1969	Royal Birkdale	Sam Snead(US) tied Eric Brown(GB)	*16-16

1971	Old Warson(St Louis)	Jay Herbert(US)	*18¹/₂-13¹/₂
1973	Muirfield(Scotland)	Jack Burke(US)	*19-13
1975	Laurel Valley	Arnold Palmer(US)	*21-11
1977	RL&A[1]	D Finsterwald(US)	*12¹/₂-7¹/₂
1979	Greenbrier	Billy Casper(US)	*17-11
1981	Walton Heath	Dave Marr(US)	*18¹/₂-9¹/₂
1983	PGA National[4]	J Nicklaus(US)	*14¹/₂-131/₂
1985	The Belfry	T Jacklin(Eur)	*16¹/₂-11¹/₂
1987	Muirfield Village	Tony Jacklin(Eur)	*15-13
1989	The Belfry	Tony Jacklin(Eur) tied Ray Floyd(US)	*14-14
1991	Kiawah Island	D Stockton(US)	*14¹/₂-13¹/₂
1993	The Belfry	Tom Watson(US)	*15-13
1995	Oak Hill	B Gallacher(Eur)	*14¹/₂-13¹/₂
1997	Valderrama	S Ballesteros(Eur)	*14¹/₂-13¹/₂
1999	Brookline	B Crenshaw(US)	*14¹/₂-13¹/₂
2002	Belfry	S Torrance(Eur)	*15¹/₂-12¹/₂

* non playing captain
**Thunderbird(Palm Springs)
[1] Eldorado(Palm Desert)
[2] Royal Lytham & St Annes
[3] Champions(Houston)
[4] PGA National(Palm Beach)

RYDER CUP RECORDS

Overall record: US 24 wins, GB/GB & Ire/Eur 7 wins, 2 ties

US home record: won 15, lost 2

GB/GB & Ire/Eur home record: won 5, lost 9, tied 2

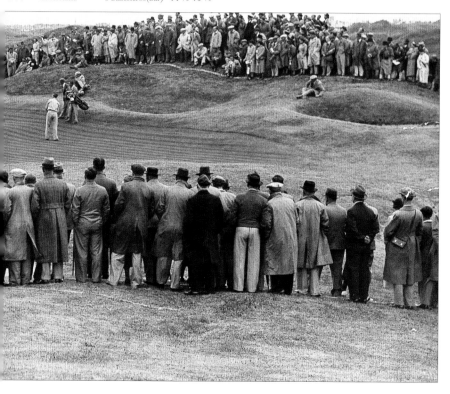

WOMEN IN GOLF

G olf may well be considered the sport of gentlemen, but it is just as popular with women, both as audience and players. The ladies circuit may not rival the men's game in media coverage, but it remains a serious professional sport in its own right. With increased corporate sponsorship, prize money on the professional tours in both the USA and Europe increased dramatically during the later half of the twentieth century, with some ladies become household names.

Perhaps the first woman of note was Mary, Queen of Scots who was reputed to have been so obsessed by golf that she was playing it just days after the murder of her husband, Lord Darnley. It was not, however, until the late nineteenth century that women began to organize themselves and play in clubs and competitions. Like the men's game, golf was a sport for genteel ladies, however they met with considerable resistance from their male counterparts. The majority of golf courses were unavailable to women an issue which exists today. Controversy surrounded the LGU (Ladies' Golf Union) decision to hold the 1984 Curtis Cup at Muirfield, a club that does not admit women members. Even the R&A is closed to women.

Social restrictions during the nineteenth century meant that the game was, in essence, a far less challenging pursuit for women. Long skirts, tight sleeves, restrictive corsets and girdles – female golfers were rarely seen raising their swing! Ladies really began to make an impression during the early decades of the twentieth century. British pioneers included players such as Cecilia Leitch who played Harold Hilton in the 'Battle of the Sexes' at Walton Heath in 1910. Her victory was only marred by the fact that she received a stroke for each alternate hole to compensate for the difference in strength. During the 1920s a number of players began to dominate the women's game. The two most important were from either side of the Atlantic: Britain's Joyce Wethered and America's Glenna Collett Vare.

Below: Mrs McNair in the 1913 English Ladies Golf Championship.
Opposite Page: Ladies' fashion c1911.

Wethered was the female equivalent of Bobby Jones. Although not formally trained, she was only a teenager when she beat Leitch in the English Amateur of 1920. She is recognized as the most talented woman golfer of all time, *Above: The 1932 US women's team prepare to meet Great Britain at Wentworth.* winning three out of five British Amateurs and was unbeaten in the English Ladies Open between 1924 and 1929. Her male counterparts considered her just as great as her female rivals and admirers included Henry Cotton and Bobby Jones.

Collett was also a natural golfer, with a passion for the game. Introduced to golf by her father, she won six US Women's Amateur Championships. On the few occasions when Collett and Wethered competed they would draw huge crowds; at St Andrews in 1929 the streets of the town fell silent as the inhabitants gathered at the Old course.

There have been a number of gifted and successful women players through the decades and during the 40s and 50s. When women's golf became professional it was dominated by Mildred 'Babe' Zaharias. She won the US Women's Amateur in 1946, the Women's British Amateur in 1947 and the US Women's Open in 1948, 1950 and 1954. Yet golf was her second sport. She took it up after retiring from an athletics career which had earned her both Olympic gold medals and world records. She was dubbed 'Babe' as a comparison to baseball star Babe Ruth, but not for her golf swing, Zaharias had excelled as a profession baseball star too!

Nancy Lopez was the star of the 1970s and during her career accumulated a number of titles, including three LPGA Championships and over 50 victories on the LPGA tour. A vivacious and bubbly personality, Lopez's success on the course encouraged larger audiences and helped to popularize the women's game even further.

At the turn of the millennium, names such as Laura Davies of Great Britain, Annika Sorenstam of Sweden, Se Ri Pak of Korea and Karrie Webb of Australia have become well known. With Sorenstam the current world number one, topping the money list at over $2million, Ladies' golf is as cosmopolitan and almost as lucrative as the men's game.

Below: In 1955, women wearing trousers were news.

117

GOLFING MISCELLANY

ETIQUETTE

Almost as crucial as the rules, etiquette on the course makes the difference between a good game of golf and an irritating one. Put simply, etiquette is showing manners and consideration during a round. Essentially these are the unwritten rules (although some, such as slow play, have become more concrete) passed on from golfer to golfer and inherited through the generations. When another golfer plays you should courteously stand at a distance, keeping quiet. Divots should always be replaced, bunkers should be raked smooth, dangerous balls should be indicated by a call of 'fore'. Walking in front of a driving golfer is not only discourteous but dangerous. For this reason, traffic lights were erected for both pedestrians and players on Granny Clark's Wynd, the road that cuts across the fairways of the 1st and 18th holes at St. Andrews.

SLOW PLAY

Then there is the issue of speed. Slow play can render the game not only boring but infuriating and tour players now face penalties if they spend too long assessing the distance, checking the wind direction, marking their cards and other such time-consuming habits. Players can find themselves in all sorts of trouble for playing too slowly: one extreme case involved two players coming to blows and finding themselves in court. Whereas in 2003, Seve Ballesteros, having been penalized for moving too slowly, refused to accept the ruling and adjusted his card, for which he was disqualified from the tournament.

Of course, no one really gets anywhere by losing their temper on the course. Shots can go horribly wrong. Roughs, water hazards, even trees can hamper a players progress but bending your club over your knee in a show of muscular frustration is always considered ungainly and unnecessary. It was Arnold Palmer who, as a young man had thrown his club into some trees in a fit of temper. His father's response was to tell him that he was ashamed of him and should he do such a thing again he would no longer teach him. The consequences of anger for Canadian golfer Richard McCulough were more dire. Following a poor shot, he struck his club against a golf cart. The shaft broke, flew through the air and fatally pierced the man's neck, severing an artery.

Opposite: In a match in 1937, Henry Cotton (4th from right) drove his ball into the car park. When it was found the vehicle had to be moved, after which Cotton calmly pitched to within a few yards of the hole.

GETTING TO GRIPS WITH THE GAME

The quest to find the perfect swing has been part of the world of golf since the beginning. The first book on how to play, *The Golfers' Manual*, was published in 1857, and it has been followed by an endless stream since.

Apart from the books, there have also been many contraptions invented to help golfers become better players - and updated versions of these are still available today. Now there are also videos - but in the end the best teachers are probably the top players themselves.

Below, Right & Opposite bottom right: A selection of the contraptions that have been invented to improve a player's swing. Opposite top: Tiger Woods shows how it's done. Opposite bottom left: The Golfcraft Monster, invented to test the swing of various clubs.

GEARING UP

Before 1880, golf clubs were slender and made of wood, with a long nose. The introduction of the 'guttie' ball, which was much harder and heavier than the 'feathery', caused heads to become shorter and broader. Towards the end of the nineteenth century iron clubs also began to appear, since they were cheaper to manufacture.

At the beginning of the twentieth century, club manufacturers began to experiment with different shapes and materials, aiming either to improve performance or just to keep abreast of changes in the way the game was played. Many of these designs were weird and wonderful - such as the club with a coil spring to speed the ball, and those with inserts of glass, rubber or rhinoceros skin on the club face. Most of these strange inventions fell by the wayside, either not finding a market, not being practical - or even being banned. Modern clubs are made of steel or graphite, with steel or titanium heads.

Opposite Page: The contents of Bernhard Langer's golf bag at the 1992 Open. During the course of the Championship he estimated he would use 60 balls and wear 24 different gloves. Fully packed his bag weight 40lbs, all carried by his caddy Peter Coleman. Below: A selection of antique golf clubs.

PLAYING BY THE RULES

The rules of golf are a complicated business, there are 34 of them, each designed to keep the game as fair and as uniform as possible. Because of the complexity of the rules (to read them is rather like deciphering the draft of a legal document) the R & A, who administer them throughout the world, with the exception of the United States and Mexico, are the recipients of hundreds of queries relating to the game. They are regularly updated and annual decisions are circulated and translated worldwide; translation itself can cause problems. Unfortunately, the more the R & A and the USGA try to simplify the rules, the more complex they become and the more complex they are, the more they contribute to nineteenth hole debate.

THE EARLY RULES

The first rules of the game were devised by the Gentlemen Golfers of Leith in 1744. In 1754, the Gentlemen had purchased a silver club, for which there would be an open competition held annually. In order to contest for the club, a set of rules were written up to ensure general agreement. The 13 'Articles and Laws in Playing at Golf' are the first recorded set of rules in the game. Those early rules form the basis of the rules used today, but of course, they are without all the clauses and sub-clauses that make the modern rules seem so impenetrable.

There are the straightforward:

• You must tee your ball within one club's length of the hole.
• Your tee must be on the ground.
• You are not to change the ball which you strike off the tee

And then there are the ambiguous:

• If your balls be found anywhere touching one another you are to lift the first ball till you play the last.
• You are not to remove stones, bones or any break club for the sake of playing your ball, except on the fair green, and that only within a club's length of your ball.
• If your ball comes among water, or any watery filth, you are at liberty to take out your ball and bringing it behind the hazard and teeing it, you may play it with any club and allow your adversary a stroke for so getting out your ball.
• If a ball be stopp'd by any person, horse or dog, or anything else, the ball so stopp'd must be played where it lyes.

- If you draw your club in order to strike and proceed so far in the stroke as to be bringing down your club; if then your club shall break in any way, it is to be accounted a stroke.

And then there is the downright puzzling:

- Neither trench, ditch or dyke made for the preservation of the links, nor the Scholar's holes or the soldier's lines shall be accounted a hazard but the ball is to be taken out, teed and play'd with any iron club.

The rules state that if your ball lands in water you may lift and drop it - but that assumes you haven't sent it right into the middle of a lake. Every year golfers lose millions of balls and a few enterprising souls have made a business from retrieving them - as well as the odd club hurled away in frustration. There is a thriving market in second-hand balls.

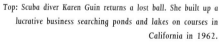

Top: Scuba diver Karen Guin returns a lost ball. She built up a lucrative business searching ponds and lakes on courses in California in 1962.
Top right: Emma Elliott-Pyle carrying out the same service in England in 1994. She estimated she could find 1,000 balls a day.
Right: Golfer Wally Edwards trained his collie, Trigger, to find balls. When he died, 10,000 were found crammed into his garden shed.

Of course, these old rules were far too general, and gradual modifications were made. All the clubs were playing to their own interpretations of these rules and with their own penalties, so in 1897 St Andrews became the arbitrary authority. Clubs are still permitted to set their own bye-laws, and often with necessity. Following the war, it was acceptable to move a ball that had finished close to an unexploded shell without incurring a penalty and a local rule in a club in mid Africa states that balls landing close to a hippopotamus or a crocodile may also be moved without penalty!

THE GREATEST SIN

The rules have evolved to become far more complex than those laid down by Leith's Gentlemen. Remember the rule, 'Your tee must be on the ground'? Rule 11.1 states, 'In teeing, the ball may be place on the ground, on an irregularity of surface created by the player on the ground or on a tee, sand or other substance in order to raise it off the ground. A player may stand outside the teeing ground to play a ball atithin it.' The R & A are clearly keen to avoid any misinterpretation, and as a result rules can contain clauses, sub-clauses, clauses of sub-clauses and additional appendices. Rule 14.3.c.i ultimately acknowledges that a golfer can wear plain gloves.

The result of such complexities means that very often, golfers take to the fairway with only the scantiest knowledge of the rules. It was Tom Watson who stated that ultimately there are only two rules: 'One play the ball as it lies. Two, if you do not know what to do next, do what you think is fair.' That second point is crucial. The majority of golfers are scrupulously fair, cheating is by far the greatest sin any player could commit, far beyond throwing one's club in anger. Unlike most sports there are no referees to adjudicate, and so the players must adhere to the rules regardless and acknowledge to officials and their opponents any breaches, whether intentional or not.

Not knowing the rules can have devastating effects on a player's overall performance. At the Dutch Open in 1992, Mike McLean lost out on winning the title when he was penalized two strokes for moving a piece of vine out of his way. It may have been a natural impediment, but it was not loose, it was attached to its roots. Likewise the rule about taking advice. The rule book states that you can only take advice from either your caddy or your partner. At the Ryder Cup in 1971, Bernard Gallacher's caddy was overheard asking Arnold Palmer's caddy what Palmer had scored, just before Gallacher took his shot. Even though Gallacher hadn't even heard the exchange, he and his partner were penalized and subsequently lost the hole. Being fastidious about the rules can work to a professional's advantage. In 1983, at the World Match Play Championship, Nick Faldo hit his ball into a group of spectators. One of the spectators, quite unacceptably, threw Faldo's ball onto the green, about 30 feet from the pin. The rules stated that Faldo should play the ball from where it lay on the green, a distinct advantage. Needless to say, Faldo's opponent was unhappy.

Just occasionally, rules that have been broken incur no penalty due to special or unusual circumstances. In 1986, four golfers on the 17th at Brora, Sutherland were forced to play their tee shots from in front of the tee, due to a cow giving birth between the markers. The Rules Committee of the R&A responded to their enquiry with the sentiment that they had played within the spirit of the game!

Opposite page: Alfred Padgham sportingly tees up for Bobby Locke at the start of their £100-a-side, 36-hole match at Selsdon Park in August 1938. Locke went on to win by two holes on the last green. Right: Ian Woosnam showing intense concentration taking a drop.

ACKNOWLEDGEMENTS

The photographs in this book are from
the archives of the *Daily Mail*.
Particular thanks to
Steve Torrington, Dave Sheppard, Brian Jackson,
Alan Pinnock, Richard Jones and all the staff.

Thanks also to
John Samuels, Cliff Salter, Maureen Hill, Alice Hill,
Marie Clayton, Carol Salter, Murray Mahon, Peter Wright,
Trevor Bunting and Mark Aris.
Design by John Dunne.